Selected other books by Robert Theobald:
The Rich and the Poor
The Challenge of Abundance
Free Men and Free Markets
The Triple Revolution:
    A Report to President Johnson (with others)
The Guaranteed Income (edited)
An Alternative Future for America
Futures Conditional
The Failure of Success (edited; with Stephanie Mills)
Economizing Abundance
Habit and Habitat
At the Crossroads (with others)

The *Rapids* of *Change*

Social Entrepreneurship in Turbulent Times

by Robert Theobald

Knowledge Systems, Inc.
Indianapolis, Indiana

Copyright © 1987 by Robert Theobald

Library of Congress Cataloging-in-Publication Data

Theobald, Robert.
    The rapids of change.

    Bibliography: p.
    Includes index.
    1. Social change. 2. Leadership. 3. Crisis management. I. Title.
HM101.T47   1987   303.4   87-3901
ISBN 0-941705-00-5
HD60 .T43 1987
Published by Knowledge Systems, Inc.
7777 West Morris Sreet, Indianapolis, Indiana 46231

Printed in the United States of America.

10 9 8 7 6 5 4 3 2 1

First Edition

With grateful thanks to

Allen Boorstein

who supported the work in the seventies

and the members of

Action Linkage

who improved this book

CONTENTS

Introduction

We live in the "rapids of change." The white waters carry us quickly on; we cannot slow down the changes coming to our culture, our society, our families, ourselves. But we do have a choice: we can learn to enjoy turbulence rather than being overwhelmed by it.

Each of us is overloaded with information and opportunities. New information which challenges our current patterns of understanding brings stress. Too much stress leads to confusion and despair. We need ways of understanding the changes that are going on so we can "think the world together" rather than "analyze it apart."

The Rapids of Change is very different from the traditional non-fiction volume. The very short sections, more like newspaper articles than chapters of a book, are designed to create an overall picture of today's realities. The book went through several drafts, each one being seen by several hundred people. Their feedback was considered at each stage of the book's development.

Problems and Possibilities

In the last fifteen years of the twentieth century, we will be confronted by more creative and more dangerous technologies, higher population density, new weapon systems, greater human competence, extraordinary crises, and insurmountable opportunities.

Already we have had a glimpse of what lies ahead. On the negative side, Chernobyl, the farm slump, international terrorism, the collapse in oil prices, the sub-Saharan famine, the Challenger disaster, the Mexico City earthquake, the Achille Lauro, and the Libyan bombing have all challenged our capacity to respond.

On the positive side, there have been the collapse in oil prices, the global Live Aid program and the U.S. Catholic encyclical on the economy, exchanges of goodwill missions between the Americans and the Russians, new patterns of workplace activities such as quality circles, and many books like *In Search of Excellence* announcing a new way of seeing the world. In addition, there have been innumerable activities on a smaller scale that show the sincere commitment of people in America and across the world. These positive actions, performed quietly by ordinary folks, do not hit the headlines, but they create a powerful counterbalance to the more dangerous public dynamics.

Many people I meet today are concerned about the negative consequences of their apparently desirable actions. They recognize the need to do more with less, to be more productive, to get rid of inefficiencies, to be entrepreneurial. They are also increasingly aware that our drive for maximum consumption and growth is resulting in unemployment, poverty, hunger, declining standards of medical care for some citizens, and a growing underclass. More and more people in decision-making positions are looking for ways to help move our culture in more favorable directions. *The Rapids of Change* provides a framework for thought about these possibilities and dilemmas.

People face very different questions depending on their roles.

• The employer must increase productivity to stay competitive, but increases unemployment as a result.

• The environmentalist wants to preserve a viable ecological system, but is forced to compromise because of society's need to provide more jobs.

• The hospital administrator needs higher efficiency, but the staff loses the time for human caring as a result.

• The educator must achieve state-mandated standards for the whole class, so is forced to ignore the uniqueness of the individual.

• The judge's inner sense of justice is compromised by having to follow precedent, even though conditions have changed.

• The military officer believes that modern weaponry is necessary to prevent war, but sees its long-run destabilizing consequences.

Few of us escape some sense of fundamental contradiction in our daily activities. If I haven't listed *your* dilemmas, take a moment to describe them for yourself. Then ask if you have worked them through, or if you have essentially abandoned all hope that you can find an approach that meets both your practical and your moral concerns.

Up to now, fundamental change issues have too often only been the concern of small, even fringe, groups. It is time these issues entered the mainstream so we can work with people who understand the need for change but don't know how to achieve it. The supportive response provided by the organizations listed in Appendix A shows how close we are to shared new understandings.

Learning New Directions

John Naisbitt has popularized the concept that the world is changing very rapidly in his book *Megatrends*. He assumes, however, that the driving forces of our time will automatically change our worldwide systems without severe trauma, and without our involvement. I am convinced that this view is unrealistic. To avoid disaster and benefit from current potentials, we must all be involved.

The drive toward human dignity and caring, part of global directions for several centuries, has come into terminal conflict with social systems based on short-run profit making, maximum efficiency, compulsive consumption and over-specialization. Our survival depends on understanding the true meaning and depth of this clash, and using the consequent conflict to support the creation of a less materialistic and more human culture. We can do this only by getting together with others to see the whole picture.

Rapids explains what has been learned about the tensions between the materialistic industrial era and our emerging "era of relationships." It provides ideas and approaches to balance our contradictions. It supports the growing effort to detail the feel of our new society, recognize the models available to create it, and identify the steps we need to take.

One helpful way to see *The Rapids of Change* is as a hologram, a three-dimensional image produced by laser technology—you have seen examples on credit cards. Holograms have one very unusual characteristic. You can cut a piece off the holographic plate; the image will be fuzzier, but the whole picture will still be there. We can imagine a sliver of the hologram which depicts our new world—this is *The Rapids of Change*. I hope you will join me, and many others, to develop larger holographic plates to make our vision of the future progressively clearer.

Alternatively, we can review the legend of the blind men and the elephant. Each blind man touched a different part of the animal and thought he knew the whole. "It's a rope!" said the one by the tail. "No, it's a snake!" said the one by the trunk.

We can imagine that somehow we've managed to give these blind men a little sight. They can now see the dim outlines of the whole elephant—but details are missing. The next challenge is to get a clearer picture. Group discussions of *Rapids* issues are one way to develop our vision: a study guide for this purpose is described in Appendix D.

Given the urgent problems that surround us, it may seem a luxury to take time to understand conditions fully before we act. Western cultures tend to demand, "Don't just sit there, do something!" Willis Harman, a well-known futurist, suggests that today we especially need to think before we make decisions. He says that we should advise people, "Don't just do something; first, sit there and understand." If society truly confronts a major crisis, we must first make sure that the steps we take will help save us, not just transfer us from the frying pan into the fire. Remember the doctor's Hippocratic Oath: "Above all, do no harm."

The Building of a New Society

What is the core of our current challenge? Our dominant societal models are based on nineteenth-century beliefs that human beings are idle, irresponsible creatures who would loaf if not controlled. Those who accept this vision, use modern technology to force higher levels of efficiency based on predetermined criteria. Through computer surveillance and statistical tracking, the performance of typists, telephone operators, and assembly line workers can be compared to a norm or to the activity of others. Efficiency can certainly be increased in this way, but is the system more *effective*? Workers trying to meet their quotas are forced to forget the need for customer service. Individual creativity and innovation are also blocked because of the incredible stress such supervision creates.

Our inherited view of human nature as "evil" is losing credibility. Some people have swung all the way and now argue that people are inherently good. They encourage people to act "naturally" without acknowledging the negative forces that also reside within us. Nor do they understand the complexities resulting from the many brain structures that have evolved during our evolutionary history.

More importantly, most of those who hold an optimistic vision of humanity fail to struggle with the question of appropriate social structures. They assume, all too often, that ideal human beings would "do good" if simply freed from all constraints. These Pollyanna images are as inadequate as our previous negative models.

The Emerging Vision

We need to start our thinking from the assumption that *healthy* human beings want to grow and to help others to grow. None of us is, however, fully effective for many reasons. We are not fully "healthy." We engage in destructive behaviors because our information is incomplete or inaccurate. We do not know how to mesh our needs and skills with other human beings or with the natural environment. In addition, the current structures of our institutions block growth and health.

All healthy organisms, from plants to animals to bioregional systems to the planet, can adapt to outside realities. Without this capacity, they would have destroyed themselves long ago. The history of the earth is full of evolutionary deadends where organisms failed to learn from experience and adapt to changing conditions.

One core question now facing us is: Will the human race be counted among the evolutionary failures? Will we recognize in time that we have moved into a new era of history and that the approaches which worked well in the past are counterproductive today?

We must change our thought and action patterns. Fortunately, the key requirements can be stated briefly and clearly.

•First, we must see conflict as a challenge to creative thinking, rather than as an excuse for violence both within and between countries.

•Second, we must learn to live within environmental and ecological limitations, rather than strive for maximum economic growth.

•Third, we must recognize that modern technology is freeing us from toil and will require profoundly different life cycles.

•Fourth, we must provide the possibility of dignity to all human beings, regardless of sex, age, race, or creed.

I can't promise unanimous agreement on ways to deal with these profound shifts. We shall certainly struggle for decades to build a just society within our greatly changed realities, once we have realized that this is the only challenge worthy of our current competence and skills. This book cannot provide all the answers, but it does pose the essential questions clearly and suggests ways to reach solutions.

The Art of Balance

What values and virtues must we strive toward? The answer is both extraordinarily old and endlessly new. It has been expressed in the core of our many world religions and spiritual traditions. It is at the heart of the golden rule. It lies behind our humanistic concerns. It is the source of our upward striving.

The language that carries our deepest beliefs must nevertheless be reinvented by each generation. Fortunately, the required new language and perceptions are now emerging. The word "good" might be replaced by "dynamic balance," and "evil" with "chaos." In essence, we should seek dynamic balance and shun chaos and breakdown.

What do I mean by balance? Think of the tennis player waiting to receive a service, the Tai-Chi expert ready to move in any direction, the caring human being ready to sense the signals from another person or group, the health professional alert to the least sign of change in a patient near a life and death crisis. These are people in balance.

We are most alive, most dynamic, when we are exquisitely in balance. Dynamic balance allows people to accomplish more than is humanly possible. It is why faith can move mountains. Balance can be expressed in many other terms. If we are religious, we can argue the need for the core values taught by prophets and preachers. If we are political analysts, we study how to recreate true democracy. If we understand system theory, we talk about the need to act on the basis of feedback and feedforward loops. But by any name, balance is the primary requirement for survival today.

The Central Paradox

We have been challenged to move toward balance since humanity first became self-conscious. Our continuing inadequacy in meeting higher potentials has led to local catastrophes. However in today's world of effectively unlimited productive and destructive power, failure to act responsibly will destroy the globe.

We need to live honestly, responsibly, humbly, and lovingly. We also need to preserve a sense of the mystery of life and accept our inability to understand reality completely. There are no absolute answers to questions, so we must listen to those who disagree with us. We must preserve a free and open society.

We must also learn to understand the true meaning of freedom. Some people argue that freedom is the right to behave the way they want. This denies all we know about individual health and societal success. Our global society has the right to demand that people behave in ways that enhance the potential for survival, but also must respect the varying conclusions about how this can best be achieved.

There are no *absolute answers*. Nobody can know for certain what the right steps are in particular situations. Freedom is possible only after we commit ourselves to understanding the need to accept fundamental diversity. The real struggle today is between the true believer who has an answer to every question and the person who has learned to live with the uncertainties of life. One of my most difficult lessons has been to accept that a true believer may not be on my side even though he or she may agree with my tentative conclusions. Our fundamental allies are those who have learned that they must continuously question and challenge themselves and others.

Our emerging culture should be life-affirming rather than life-destroying, but the necessary, specific steps to reach this goal may never be fully clear. People who appreciate the complexity of the world's situation will therefore never force their approach on others because they cannot be certain what will be best.

For example, if all the children who could be conceived were born, the world would rapidly become unbearably overpopulated. Which of us can be certain that our preferred route to cope with this reality is the best one?

Similarly, we know that doctors can now delay death until life becomes a burden both to dying individuals and those who care for them. Who among us can be sure how to respond to this challenge? If we are religious, we must accept that we now have the ability to delay death using powers we previously believed belonged only to God. We need to be humble in our attempts to wield such terrifying power. Even if we see the issue in secular terms only, the problems of cost and pain and manipulation confront us on all sides..

Similar dilemmas exist in the environmental area, where almost everybody would agree, at least in principle, that we have the responsibility to ensure a permanently viable ecology. As the evidence of increases in CO_2 levels and depletion of the ozone layer is confirmed, the need for hard choices becomes clearer.

This tension—between the unarguable need for mature individuals in a new cultural setting, and our inability to state clearly required policies—runs through this book. It is clear that new directions are required. It is also clear that the method of achieving them remains profoundly uncertain. To repeat, there are no absolute answers to real-life questions. We live in process, searching for the next steps which can move us forward. *Rapids* offers a way to examine our values and to look at desirable directions as individuals and in groups. We can then decide what we need to hold onto and what we must let go of as we run the rapids of change.

A Personal Note

Many people find it easier to read a book if they have some idea of the history of the author. The next few paragraphs will give you a sense of my personal journey. But before we get to this point you need an interpretation of the way the first personal singular is used in this book.

The word "I" in Western and American culture normally makes people think about an individual who is separate from others. My perception is quite different. I recognize that I am the sum total of my experiences—genetic, family, community, and cultural—and that anything I know is part of a larger thought stream which I only partially express.

I was born in India in 1929 and have also lived in Great Britain, France, and on the East Coast of the United States. I am now based in Wickenburg, Arizona and Dingwall, Scotland. Over the last thirty years, I have chosen to center my life within the issues discussed in this book. I am not an expert, however; indeed, there are no experts. But I have spent more time listening to individuals and groups reflect on these issues than most people have been able to devote to them

I started my work in the late fifties, arguing that the poor countries should not follow the path which the rich countries had taken during the industrial era. We are now beginning to understand why this is true, but we have lost much ground in recent decades as poor countries have accepted ineffective development processes.

My work in the early sixties centered around the inevitability of fundamental change. *The Challenge of Abundance* and *Free Men and Free Markets* showed that massive shifts were inevitable before the end of the century. A pamphlet entitled *The Triple Revolution* was created by a group of us and sent to President Johnson in 1964. Its thesis that the weaponry, computer, and human rights revolutions were destroying industrial era patterns received very heavy coverage.

During most of the sixties I lived in New York City, although it sometimes seemed as though I was perpetually on the road. I did a great deal of speaking, particularly to college audiences. I was caught up in the excitement of this period. Those of us espousing change at this time were challenging to listen to, but I now realize that there was no expectation that we could really alter reality fundamentally.

In the late sixties and early seventies my work shifted toward communication issues. Given the need for fundamental change, how could people learn the new realities? A group of us developed non-threatening models and styles so people could grow into new ways of thinking and behaving. But the seventies often seemed discouraging. Many people were afraid of the future, hoping that the problems and crises would just go away.

The last ten years have kept me busy with many projects. Some of the more interesting challenges were with the Congressional Office of Technology Assessment on energy usage, with Control Data Corporation on its advanced PLATO computer, with the U.S. Department of Agriculture on alternative futures, and with the State of Nebraska on new visions and citizen involvement. I have also been struggling to find a way to communicate what I have learned over the previous three decades. This, after many false starts, resulted in *At the Crossroads*, a pamphlet published in 1984, and this book. Behind all this work has been a commitment to helping people cope with the consequences of profound uncertainty.

For the last seventeen years, I have been developing a network of people who share a belief in our capacity to use today's fundamental changes to create a better society. The network has gone through many shifts. At an early date it consisted of about 100 people receiving mailings from me.

Later it was a trendletter called *Futures Conditional* with a circulation of over 1,000. Later still it became *Action Linkage*, our current name. We are a group of some 800 people working together to discover and create positive processes and directions for our society. We are concerned with ideas and knowledge that will help us act to create a higher quality of life throughout the world. There's more information about Action Linkage in Appendix D.

How should you evaluate *The Rapids of Change*? You should take nothing on faith, of course, because as I have already said, there are no experts. I have tried to signal where I personally feel certain by using the words "must," "need to," and other similar phrases. I have avoided them elsewhere.

We already know a great deal more about the questions we must face than has been accepted by our world culture. Some of my more challenging, and even distressing, issues fall in this category. It is not always pleasant to face reality. Failing to do so, however, will be even more distressing, given the penalties that now exist if we persist in our current patterns.

Some changes are now clearly required for our survival: but how we should make the transition and what the new world will look like is still profoundly uncertain.

The Structure of the Book

There are seven parts to the book; you may want to read them in different order depending on what you already know.

Section 1: *The Images of Change* provides a context for thinking about discontinuities. This is a good starting point for those who sense the breakdown of our society but do not yet have images to explain it.

Section 2: *Beyond the Rapids* explains the emerging vision of a healthy society. It is a good starting point for those who can already explain what is going on and are sorting out what directions make sense.

Section 3: *Leadership Patterns in the Rapids* discusses the change in leadership styles from "power over" to "power with." It is a good starting point for those who can explain what is going on and what they want to achieve, but are not as effective in their actions as they would like to be.

Section 4: *The Scales of Change* explores the scales of change starting at the individual leadership level and moving to the global. People interested in a particular pattern of action may choose to start here, but will usually benefit from reading Section 3 first.

Section 5: *The Skills of Change* uses a set of short provocative statements to talk about our behavior patterns. It is the most impressionistic part of the book and will be a good starting point for those who want to create more effective personal styles.

Section 6: *Managers of Crisis* argues that current dangers, particularly our economic breakdowns, can be turned into positive opportunities. It is a good starting point for those who are seeking leverage points to change our culture in positive directions.

Section 7: *Putting It All Together* pulls the argument together, showing how we usually search for super-sophisticated answers to super-obsolete questions. It provides models and tools for continued activity after you finish reading the book.

I have assumed that most readers who read this book want to get an overview of what is happening, learn where we are going, and then decide what *you* can do about it. In this case, you will get most out of the book if it is read in the order presented.

This is a work in progress. It has been developed to this point by many people who have contributed their skills and imagination. You are invited to help us take the next steps. Please read the appendices and get in touch with us if you want to be involved.   OOO

Acknowledgements

My thanks go to those who have taught me over the last thirty years, particularly my wife Jeanne Scott, and also to the many members of Action Linkage. More specifically, I need to thank Ann Weiser in San Francisco, and Joan and Art Meen in Wickenburg, who made sure I completed the book. Finally, my thanks go to the investors who believed in *Rapids* enough so that it could be launched with imagination and flair through a new company called Knowledge Systems, Inc.

This book is a summary of work done by many individuals and groups. I have paid them the ultimate compliment of forgetting who has taught me what. I have used their knowledge and wisdom in my own work and now hope to share it with you.

SECTION 1

The Images
of Change

Your world is unique. And so is mine. Each of us sees reality through our own individual perceptions.

These perceptions are heavily affected by our cultural and societal traditions. The pace of change in technology and knowledge systems has, however, outdated much of our past understandings. We need to look afresh at the realities that surround us.

This part of Rapids aims to provide an overview of our emerging compassionate era. I hope the material will support you in your own learning path, even though you may not accept or agree with everything I have written.

We are moving through rapid and discontinuous changes. We need new skills which we can discover together. Welcome to our journey through the rapids.

The Rapids of Change

We are being swept downstream by a torrent of change. Each year, each month, and almost every week, the landscape alters. The familiar vanishes, and with it the effectiveness of the ways we have made decisions as individuals, families, groups, and communities.

This is the overwhelming reality of our times. It challenges us at every level. It destroys the validity of traditional patterns of behavior.

We have shifted into these rapids without really noticing them. We are driven by the weaponry, biology, and human rights revolutions, by computers and ecological limitations. Nevertheless, some people are still acting as though they are on a slow-running river and can afford to relax. Others have recognized that everybody else is in the rapids but act as though they can be spectators, watching while people drown.

In reality, the white water around all of us makes it urgent that we discover how to respond. A growing number are learning to enjoy the turbulent pace. But many are so frightened that they are unable to take any steps to save themselves. A few scream at the top of their voices, making their fellow passengers even more terrified.

We cannot predict our course through the rapids. Held by the current, we must respond, almost instinctively, as we see rocks appearing ahead.

We need new and creative responses to meet our growing crises. Unfortunately, many still refuse to see that the world has changed. Most politicians and academics still argue that the extraordinary economic successes of the twenty-five post-World War II years, from 1945-1970, can continue. They deny that the current is stronger than any force we can muster.

Some have suggested that we are already living through World War III. This image obviously has major flaws, but it helps us understand the degree of military, political, cultural, and economic violence in the world. Major clashes have developed between various points of views, both in different parts of national societies and between countries.

Survival requires that we go with the flow rather than fight against it. So we need to accept change and make it our friend. This can be a wonderful time to be alive as humanity struggles out of its adolescence and moves toward maturity. But only by anticipating future changes can we achieve maturity.

Trend is not destiny. If, in the sixties, we had recognized the dramatic impact of computers and robots on work, income, and organization, we would have had more options in the eighties. Similarly, if we determine the impact of the biological revolution in the eighties, we shall seize more of the potentials and avoid more of the problems in the nineties.

But with greater knowledge comes greater responsibility. Now our most profound perceptions of what we can do to, for, and with the human being are being altered. If we are to keep up with our ever-increasing power, we need to apply our ethical values. It is no longer enough to provide information to people who are searching for new responses to emerging questions: we need to develop knowledge systems which help people make ethical decisions in a complex and interdependent world.

The human race is now shaping its own future. Given the complexities of our time, optimism is unrealistic. But despair is also useless because it saps courage and prevents action. We need to develop realistic hope which recognizes that crises are inevitable but they can be times of great opportunity.

The river we are travelling divides not so far ahead: one side goes over a high waterfall which portends the destruction of our world. Unless we learn how to manage our productive and destructive powers, chaos will develop and our chances of survival will be slim.

The other side of the river continues down through the rapids but settles into calmer water ahead. First, we must avoid the waterfall by creating new cultural and socioeconomic models which recognize the need for profound diversity. Then using these models, we can aim for the gentler currents.

To reach the gentle currents, we must put our most competent people where they can be effective. Some will steer, some will comfort the weak, some will manage supplies. A few will act as scouts, helping us choose the appropriate channel down the river.

Our crew must include servant leaders who recognize not only their abilities but also their limitations. Our process for managing change should involve many people of diverse talents rather than treating most citizens as passive observers.

Above all, we need to make decisions on the basis of the fundamental values common to traditions around the world. We need to be honest, responsible, loving, and humble and to recognize that there will always be issues which we cannot understand or control.

Leadership in the rapids requires very different skills than we have needed in more stable times. Discovering these new leadership skills is at the heart of the challenge we face today.   OOO

The Driving Forces

Many forces are affecting the future and causing it to change in both predictable and unpredictable ways. These driving forces are so well established that they will continue to affect events and trends for years, and even decades, into the future. Good decision-making requires that we recognize these trends and factor them into our discussions. Eight key forces are listed below:

1. *The weaponry revolution.* Modern weaponry—chemical, biological and nuclear —cannot be abolished in any foreseeable future. War is therefore no longer an acceptable means to resolve conflict. We must abandon the belief that we can permit conflict to cause violence. Rather we must find ways to use conflict to create new patterns which will benefit all those involved. We must learn how to use conflict to spark imagination rather than anger. This is true not only nationally and internationally, but also in families, communities, and between groups such as labor and management

2. *The computer and robot revolution.* The industrial revolution progressively removed the need for muscle power and replaced it with machines. Similarly, the computer revolution now taking place will replace repetitive mental activity. Some fear that these machines will replace people; however, there is no reason to assume that machines will deal with the future better than we can. Indeed, at the moment, machines are excluded by their very design from the complex and emotional decision-making which is required to meet the challenge of the future.

3. *The environmental revolution.* There are obvious limits to the amount of abuse the global environment can absorb. Small areas have, of course, been destroyed by bad husbandry many times in human history. But today we know that current human activities are changing even the global climate, although the extent, and even the direction

of the change, continues to cause strong argument. Because we cannot predict the impact of large-scale ecological or climatological change, we must limit as much as possible the changes caused by man-made wastes. This demands, in turn, that we abandon our drive toward maximum economic growth, learning to balance the negative effects of pollution with the very real need for an increased standard of living in many parts of the world.

4. *The human rights revolution.* Certain classes of people have held power and authority over others throughout human history. Privileges have been granted because people belonged to a particular race, sex, income level, or age group. We are now learning that everybody should be treated with respect and should have the right to live with dignity. The sweep of this human rights revolution is changing our world profoundly. Some contemplate its reversal, but it is improbable that people will accept such a curtailment of their hopes for a dignified life.

5. *Population.* World population continues to increase. While the percentage rate of increase in human population has declined, the absolute number of people on the globe continues to rise more rapidly than ever before. Cutting this increase will not be easy because so many young people in the poor countries still have their child-bearing years before them. The pattern in the rich countries is very different: some nations have zero population growth. As a result, the population in the rich countries is aging rapidly.

6. *Migration.* In the poor countries, large numbers of people are moving from the rural areas to the cities. Current estimates suggest that by the year 2000, eight of the ten largest cities in the world will be in the developing nations. The 1985 earthquake in Mexico City showed the type of crisis which will emerge if this growth continues unchecked. That natural disaster's effects were intensified by overcrowded conditions in substandard housing, which collapsed during the quake. Overpopulation, poverty, and political oppression have led millions of citizens in poor countries to "vote

with their feet" by moving into richer nations. This trend is most evident along the Mexican-U.S. border. As this flood of immigration probably cannot be controlled, the character of Texas, New Mexico, Arizona, and Southern California will be dramatically altered.

7. *Biology*. We are developing the capacity to re-design plants, animals, and human beings. But these skills will pose some of the most severe challenges we face. At one level, biotechnology will dramatically alter the agricultural sector of the economy as new breeds of plants and animals are created in far less time. Even more critically, new techniques will give us power over our own evolution. To manage this responsibility, we shall need far more wisdom than we have currently shown .

8. *Knowledge systems*. Perhaps the most dramatic, if the least visible of all the driving forces, is the shift in the ways in which we think and structure knowledge. The industrial era fragmented reality by encouraging the division of labor and information. Our new era is pulling it together again: everything both is, and is increasingly seen to be, interconnected. Today the world is a twenty-four hour marketplace for goods and services, and a resonating sounding board for news events. Interconnecting life audiences by video is an example of positive potentials. The increasingly severe clash of competitive world views is our major danger.

Today's driving forces create the rapids of change. Because they interact in unpredictable ways, we cannot control the future fully. So we must learn to live *in the moment*, with a profound sense of both the past that has made us and the future we can create by our actions. We are responsible both for avoiding the immediate dangers and for building a society which will learn to act before crises overwhelm us.

OOO

Living with Discontinuities

Most people in Western societies still act as though the future can be predicted from the past. Technically, this is known as an "extrapolist model" of reality.

Extrapolist models have served the West relatively well until now. During both short-term and long-term economic cycles, growth has continued and the standard of living for the average person within the rich countries has always risen over time. Today, however, we can identify a pattern of fundamental discontinuities which is rapidly shifting all the old rules and understandings. The future will be profoundly different from the past, and the old models won't work.

For example, before the oil shocks of the seventies, economists assumed that energy usage would continue to climb without limit. But over the last fifteen years, demand actually declined. Lower demand then led to dramatic declines in oil prices in 1986; these cheaper prices, in turn, will also cause fundamental and unexpected shifts over the next few years.

When changes occur today, most analysts try to determine whether they are good or bad. This analysis ignores the primary danger of our times: that the pace, intensity, and frequency of shifts are shaking our socioeconomic system apart. The resulting uncertainty is so great that more and more individuals and groups are paralyzed.

The level of confusion is increased because most people still assume that changes are continuous rather than jerky and unexpected. Gregory Bateson, a highly challenging British anthropologist and systems analyst, was one of the first to show that discontinuities are common in human, social, and biological systems. Even the geological record demonstrates this pattern of unexpected change. Long periods of stability are followed by shorter periods of relatively dramatic change in the earth's structure. Similarly, climatologists have discovered that sharp shifts in climate can occur in a few years.

In all areas, cultural systems that seem quite stable may shift far more rapidly than anybody believes possible. For example, the Meiji Revolution in Japan in the 1840's swept away the Samurai, who had seemed firmly established as the nation's power structure. The change was brutal and sudden, taking only a few years. But even profound shifts do require preparation. Changes in patterns of thought and action always take time, but most people fail to see the evidence until the shift finally happens. Those who ignore the warning signs are ambushed by new developments.

A society that has been successful in one period of history is often oblivious to new patterns. So cultures confronted with excessive change often collapses Alternatively, it will look for a man on a white horse or a strong religious leader to relieve people of their fear and confusion. History abounds with these patterns; in modern times, Ayatollah Khomeini's Iran serves as a graphic example of a society surrendering to a religious despot.

Some argue that Western societies have grown beyond such dangers, that "it cannot happen here." But those who study the growing power and influence of extreme groups throughout the rich world agree that such a view ignores reality.

It is all too easy to write a scenario about the way in which a fascist system could emerge here in the affluent West. Robert Heinlein centered his novel *Revolt in 2100.* around the possibility of a repressive dictatorship in the United States. Betram Gross coined the term *Friendly Fascism.* to use as the title of his book to describe a world in which modern social science and communications technology enable control to be exercised without obvious repression and violence.

The only way to avoid the threat of dictatorship is to teach people to understand realities and manage their own destiny. There are no shortcuts to maturity. Each of us now has to learn to live in a world of profound uncertainty. We shall need new knowledge systems to support the shift into a future which cannot be fully defined. And we must recognize that change is the only constant and that we should be its creative agents.

We are choosing between two futures: one threatens repression; the other offers openness. We must take Thomas Jefferson's adage to heart: "I know of no safe depository of the ultimate powers of the society but the people themselves; and if we think them not enlightened enough to exercise their control with a wholesome discretion, the remedy is not to take it from them, but to inform their discretion by education." Active citizenship today is not a luxury but a necessity, and we must be educated to achieve it.   ○○○

Experiencing the Rapids

Few of us spend much time analyzing the rapids of change theoretically and analytically. Rather our emotions are tugged and pulled as old relationships shift and change in the turbulence. This uncertainty affects our most basic connections, as staying related to other human beings is difficult without clear guidelines. Now we do not even know the rules for relationships. We do not agree on how men and women will relate, employers and employees, or parents and children. As a result, we no longer know how to organize churches, schools, nonprofit groups, or businesses effectively. Everything is in flux.

Our problems are made more difficult because the more valuable the relationship, the harder it is to avoid "running a tape." We get caught in patterns which have proved destructive in the past, but we do not know how to escape from them. This can occur within relationships as husbands and wives replay past angers or between generations as battered children turn into abusive parents. A trigger stimulus sets off a repetitive response and the whole miserable experience is relived once more.

Two fundamental choices are open to us in this time of stress and tension and trauma. On the one hand, we are being invited back to the apparent security of the industrial era and the "good old times." Fundamentalist churches and extreme right-wing leaders argue that we can still solve problems as we always did. The good old times, however, were never as good as they now seem in retrospect. Re-creating them would be a fatal error because they cannot deal with today's driving forces.

The alternative approach is to put our efforts into understanding the turbulence of our times and attempting to pass through it using new approaches. Can we understand what is going on and can we do something about it? The clashes and turbulence we are now experiencing emerge because new problems and possibilities are created as we learn to understand and control more of our universe. For example, the birth of a damaged or deformed baby in the old days was seen as a tragic Act of God. Now we can often trace the causes of natal problems, and therefore we face new choices.

For example, we have learned that a mother's behavior during her pregnancy can affect her child. Now a legal movement is developing to punish mothers whose bad habits during pregnancy, such as drug abuse, caused their children difficulties after birth. How far can such a movement go without interfering with human choice and civil liberties? The grief and anger on all sides of these questions is genuine. How can we be fair and reasonable to all parties?

In this particular issue, the difficulty goes very deep. Our most intractable arguments emerge when both sides have "right" on their side. While a child has a right to the best possible start in life, a woman also has a right to choose her own behavior. And we cannot be sure that a mother's habits were the cause of the child's problems. In addition, we know from hard experience the dangers of permitting the state to intervene in private decision-making.

Another conflict of values is emerging in the field of education. Western cultures have been committed to exposing children to a broad range of behavior patterns and beliefs. But a growing number of fundamentalist groups demand that their children's experience should be narrowed to cover only what *they* believe and find appropriate. Both of these approaches "make sense" within the contexts used for thought and analysis. Can a compromise be found?

A third very difficult issue is our growing knowledge of genetic structures, which may let us predict on a statistical basis the probability of certain individuals committing crimes. Should society make any use of this knowledge and, if so, how? Most people support crime prevention in this violent age. But individuals are not statistics: they have free will and the capacity for molding their future. Again, the conflict between societal and individual values can prevent intelligent choice.

An issue most Americans are facing is the sudden change in marriage patterns. Previously, the most visible style for marriage was that of the dominant, breadwinning male and the submissive, homemaking female. As women move into the workforce, that pattern changes, and our overall vision of healthy relationships shifts. The industrial-era vision of marriage is increasingly obsolete. What marriage models will work in the future? How can stress be limited as this shift in styles takes place?

Finally, we need only remember that war and violence have always been the method for settling international conflict. But war is now too dangerous. We need profoundly different strategies for dealing with conflict, both internally and internationally.

How can we pick our way through these and many other minefields which, in real life, never occur clearly or unemotionally? Two elements will permit us to make a more effective response. First, we must learn where the rapids are taking us. This is one primary purpose of this book. Hopefully, after completing it, you'll have a better sense of what issues are foreclosed by the driving forces, and what choices are open to us.

The second need, however, is to learn to live in a world of diversity. This requires that we recognize that several people confronting the same situation will see *profoundly* different pictures and that they will all be valid at the level of individual experience. Examining *Rapids* issues with a diverse group of people is one way to understand just how differently reality can be seen by various people and groups.

Finally, we all need to learn how our individual understandings can be meshed into a broader, deeper, and more relevant picture. An individual's own vision is the only pattern one can see at any moment in time, but it is inevitably limited and partially false. Each of us must join with others to discover a more comprehensive reality.

We must learn to be passionate about our beliefs without denying the passions of others. Strong beliefs, in the past, have almost always been intolerant. Today we need tolerant passion and compassion. Working from the best ideas one has, while remaining open to new thoughts, requires the maintenance of a dynamic balance.   OOO

Becoming a Change Agent

I can trace my concern about change to an interview with one of my professors at Harvard University. I went into the office of the Dean of the Graduate School of Public Administration and offered some ideas I thought new and interesting. His response was, "If the ideas are new, they are not important. If they are important, then they are not new."

I was young and naive and therefore felt I had been treated unreasonably. Actually, I had received the best possible introduction to the difficulties of altering people's vision and perception. Systems and people inevitably resist change. This resistance is a survival factor. If people accepted all new input uncritically, their behavior would change continuously and they would be impossible to live or work with. Those of us who want to be effective change agents must cease to rail against the difficulty of change. Instead, we must understand the importance of stability in the survival of people and systems. In this period of rapid change, we must maintain the old wherever we can, so as to give people a sense of continuity.

This is why historic preservation is so critical. My wife, Jeanne Scott, is our town historian. Although our community is only about 125 years old, valuing its past gives people a sense of rootedness not available in any other way. The ability to create the future is profoundly based in a sense of continuity from the past.

When my wife and I wrote our science-fiction book, *Teg's 1994*, we lived near a building which had originally been a monastery. When the challenges of the future seemed too great, the ruins reminded us of the many apparently insuperable problems humanity had survived.

Being effective in today's world requires that we filter and screen the incredible amount of stimuli that exists. We would destroy ourselves if we tried to look at all the available information and take advantage of every opportunity. Our conscious and unconscious patterns fortunately already limit our input. Still, most of us need to be more effective in keeping out unwanted signals. This is why institutions and knowledge systems control the influx of information.

Problems develop, however, when our screens work to maintain old realities and to keep out new knowledge needed for intelligent action. Our formal education processes do not teach how to find new directions. Fortunately, today we are aware of, and can teach, communication skills that enable people to see reality more easily. Here are a few of them:

•People need to be aware of the patterns of perception created by their individual and group past and those of others. People who come from particular states, countries, professions, and communities have unique ways of looking at reality; so do different age groups, classes, and genders. These thought structures help determine what ideas people find acceptable and, even more critically, the language and concepts that can be effectively used to communicate new ones. Change agents must work within the current thinking of a person or group so that new approaches mesh effectively with current understandings.

•People must develop a vision of the future which will challenge them to be active and creative. Those who have worked with communities and individuals find that most groups and people normally start with quite limited ideas about what would be desirable. Nevertheless, the first step must be to meet people's existing hopes. When people see they can bring about change, they can be challenged to accept broader goals. They can also be shown that their intended route into the future may not produce the gains they hope to achieve.

•Showing that immediately felt needs can be met is essential. The primary block to effective action, in all too many cases, is a pervasive sense of powerlessness. People need to learn they have the potential to change their future. Once empowerment has occurred, they will be willing to strive toward a clearly articulated, broadly shared vision.

Most people alter very slowly the models within which they think and learn. Stability in ideas and concepts has helped people and institutions survive throughout history, so resistance to change can be expected. The need for "change agents" or "social entrepreneurs"—people who have the skills and are willing to take the risks involved in bringing new ideas to individuals, groups, and institutions—is therefore critical. And since the traditional model of "killing the messenger who brings the bad news" is not far behind us, we must provide those change agents with human and financial support systems.

What is a social entrepreneur or change agent? Joseph Schumpeter, an Austrian economist, described entrepreneurs as unafraid of the fact that very few things worth doing would be undertaken on a sober calculation of the odds. Western cultures have become accustomed to economic entrepreneurs, and we accept change that satisfies our economic wants. We do not yet effectively support social entrepreneurs, who help people discover new ways of creating a high quality of life.   OOO

Working as a Change Agent

We need to develop a profoundly different vision of creative behavior. I suspect that social entrepreneurs and change agents are today widely seen as "loud mouths with causes." In my experience, they are also predominantly perceived as being on the left of the political spectrum and as trying to force new views, patterns, and policies on the culture. The decline of the left in American politics has largely destroyed the credibility of this form of activity.

Surprisingly, right-wing activists are not often seen as change agents. This seems to be due to the belief that the right wing is simply trying to restore the past, to get back to previously existing conditions. The problem with this reasoning is that the world has changed so dramatically that restoring past models may be the most negative step we can possibly take because old styles often will not fit new realities.

Both left-wing and right-wing change agents tend to have one behavior trait in common: they are true believers. They are convinced that if the society would only accept their particular answer or set of answers, our problems would vanish or at least be greatly reduced.

Those of us who have been in the change business since the nineteen-fifties and sixties—or even earlier—are learning an extraordinarily difficult lesson. In the past, our allies were those people who shared our conclusions and our commitments to specific causes. We worked with those who were willing to demonstrate their demand for the changes which we saw as positive. We are discovering today that all issues are interconnected and that tackling one problem at a time can be profoundly counterproductive.

Today, we are learning that our allies are those who are prepared to listen to all voices in the world, not just their own. We are working with those who see the richness of all our cultures and draw creativity and imagination out of differences. We are slowly and painfully coming to understand that sharing the conclusions of another person is not the touchstone. Rather it is the mutual commitment to dialogue and "open space."

This is a difficult change to absorb and one we are all struggling to understand. The bottom line of our work is no longer converting others to a particular point of view, but encouraging commitment and will, so that we shall all learn how to search for positive changes. Activities designed to create enthusiasm and willpower require very different techniques from those which are effective in changing only attitudes toward policies. We have to struggle with the issue of personal empowerment and what it takes to convince people that their actions and leadership can make a difference.

We can indirectly reach an understanding of what we need to do by examining the implications of one of the smaller patterns which developed on the day of President Kennedy's assassination. A group of social scientists had been dropping wallets in the street, charting the patterns which emerged as some wallets were returned and some were kept by the finders. The percentage returned had been reasonably stable until the day of Kennedy's death, when not one wallet was returned.

The hypothesis developed from this startling result was that people felt that the world owed them something to make up for the tragedy, and that they were therefore entitled to the wallet they found. Over the next years, this thesis was tested exhaustively. People were exposed to good and bad news before being asked to make decisions. The openness, caring, and creativity of the subjects' decisions correlated with the type of news they were fed.

The implications of this research study for the work of today's change agents are obvious. If we want people to respond positively to opportunities and challenges, we must help them move beyond despair and see the realistic reasons for hope. The current barrage of negative images on TV, both in the news and in entertainment, reduce our potential to bring about positive change. Positive images, on the other hand, should increase that potential.

Positive and negative energy does spread. Visualizations of hopeful futures will help bring them into existence, both in personal lives and in societies. Positive change can only happen as we alter our visions of what we want to achieve and as we commit ourselves to creative activities.

This is the individual and personal side of the change process. But we must also achieve a mesh with our social and community needs, and direct our communal energy towards the future. If people gather energy around outdated directions and goals, they will inevitably drive the society and culture in the wrong direction.

The thesis of *Rapids* is that essentially all our industrial-era goals are obsolete, and that we must therefore help potential leaders discover new directions. Section 2 of this book takes up many of the most urgent shifts. However, before we can move onto specific directions for change, we must look at the implications of our increasingly complex, interdependent, and diverse world.

The fundamental patterns of the industrial era assumed that it made sense to make people feel and react alike. We aimed to limit individuality so people could fit into machine-like systems. In contrast, the central need of our emerging era is to find ways to use the diverse strengths of each individual and to manage the weaknesses. This point has been made most vigorously and clearly by those trying to change business practices so each of us have the opportunity to use our skills and creativity in any work we do. This

vision of greater human potential is now spreading throughout the culture. What are the implications of this shift for
the world in which we shall live? How can we manage
radical diversity?   OOO

Discovering Diversity

Most of us are familiar with various perceptual tests that
demonstrate how we see the world according to our personal understandings. For example, engineers rarely, if ever, see
people when they look at Rorschach ink-blot tests. Social
workers, on the other hand, are likely to discover faces and
bodies.

Even though we "know" that perceptions are controlled
by our genetics and experience, much current work and communication continues to be based on the belief that we shall
eventually find an objective perspective from which to
analyze reality. Most intellectual and academic analysis fails
to recognize that today's so-called objective perspective is
merely our Western view, which is challenged by other
philosophical understandings and even our own most
recent thinking.

Unfortunately, those who move beyond Western "objectivity" often find themselves mired in absolute subjectivity.
People who abandon the belief in *one* "right" view may
come to accept *all* understandings as equally valid. The benefits from diversity are then lost in confusion.

People inevitably experience and hence perceive different parts of our complex reality. For example, Europeans
like me, who were born before 1935 are indelibly marked by
the experience of the Second World War. It was so critical to
our thought patterns that, even forty years after its end, we
find it hard to remember that the vast majority of the
world's population today see World War II as history.

Detective stories have taught us that each person's finger-prints are unique. It is time we learned that each person's patterns of thought and behavior are also unique. We must find ways to make a world based on fundamental diversity in perception exciting and effective rather than confusing. Fortunately, there are ways to limit disagreements and misunderstandings between those holding different subjective views.

During the industrial era, we tried to deny diversity. We acted in ways that decreased or destroyed the uniqueness of the individual. We are now learning that systems operate optimally when we create a dynamic mesh maximizing the strengths and minimizing the weaknesses of individuals.

The French have a saying that everybody has the weak-nesses of their strengths. For example, a healthily dominant person may become arrogant in certain conditions. A caring person may break down under excessive stress. The proverb is equally revealing when it is reversed, showing that people have the strengths of their weaknesses. The good manager gets people to work together in ways which ensure that inevitable human conflicts are constructive rather than destructive in their results.

Effective systems depend on three patterns. *First*, people must share purpose and direction, or otherwise they will not work together effectively. Organizations that function well always have shared commitments, not all of which are rational. Typically, successful groups have a rich fund of inside jokes and anecdotes, which bind them together and enable them to get through the hard times that are part of any organization's or community's life-cycle.

Of course, there is often a major tension between the needs of workers for internal cohesion and the requirement of an organization to achieve its goals. A good organization balances its own needs with care for the people within it. It uses the diversity of its workers to help them see what is going on and what needs to be changed. Managers in these organizations don't fear negative feedback because they know they can benefit from it.

The *second* requirement for an effective group is the ability to perceive new realities Developing a sense of shared purpose is one of the best ways to prevent the development of closed systems and ideologies. So long as people are clear about what they are trying to do, they are likely to observe the outside environment in order to increase their effectiveness. On the other hand, groups that are working together only because there is a paycheck to be earned are far less likely to do more than their job.

Third, an effective organization must be adept at implementing action plans. Balancing the process of rethinking directions to keep up with constant change against the need for stability is currently one of our most difficult problems. Projects and goals must at some point be given final form to permit action. Knowing when to do this is a key to success in our rapidly changing world. But there are ominous signs that the level of uncertainty in the world is becoming so great, it may come to prevent effective individual and organizational actions.

The central task in a perceptual universe is to keep yourself in balance. You can then learn most creatively and teach most responsibly. Believing that you can lead using power and position is one of the assumptions of the objective world. Leadership in our emerging era must be based on competence and knowledge. The concept that some people are teachers and others learners will be replaced by the idea that we are always both teachers and learners.

There is no certainty in a perceptual universe; we can never be sure what we should do. Paradoxically, being excited by this reality is one major challenge of our emerging era. One of the primary roles of today's change agents and social entrepreneurs is to support institutional renewal in a way which ensures creative and imaginative conflict. This is very different from past processes, which aimed to create a monolithic system where disagreement was barely tolerated at best and harshly suppressed at worst.   OOO

Living with Diversity

Do we control our future? This is one of the most diffi-cult questions in theology and philosophy. Some believe that our actions have no effect on our destiny, while others think that there are no constraints on human potential. And still others assume that the course of events is basically inflexible most of the time, but that shifts are sometimes possible. As editor of the book *Futures Conditional*, I used three science-fiction stories to dramatize the viewpoints about the flexibility of the past and the future.

One story portrays a hunting party which goes back into the remote past and kills a butterfly by mistake. When the party returns to their own time, they discover that as a result of their action their world has changed, radically, for the worse. This story dramatizes the view that all events are important and that even the most trivial action can cause major shifts in directions.

Another story has a couple travelling on a train and meeting a person with a "what if" box, which lets them see what would have happened had they not met when they did. They discover that they would not have been wed in the same circumstances, but would have been married and on the same train by the time the story takes place. This ap-proach illustrates the belief that changing the course of history is very difficult.

In the third story, a time-travel war party moves back into the past at what they assume to be a critical moment. By altering the movements of a key player, they change the out-come of a battle. The assumption is that there are certain moments in history when fundamental change is particular-ly possible.

The thesis of *Rapids* is that we are living in one of these moments. It will not, however, be a single great hero or heroine who causes the required changes. But rather a sig-nificant number of people will see a need for a new pattern and set out to create it through making a very *large* number of *small* changes. In fact, we are already further along in achieving the necessary changes than is generally realized. The effective alterations that are taking place are, however, hidden by the diversity in our society. While the efforts of many groups are converging toward a new system, their fundamental agreement is difficult to see and their conflicts are often obvious. This apparent lack of a shared vision discourages many of us from making a major leadership commitment.

We need the confidence—and the skills—to help in the process of changing the society. We need to support the role of the citizen-leader rather than the large-scale hero. Too many of us still hope that a leader, several times larger than life, will come along. We are impatient with the small-scale shifts that take place throughout the society as a result of the efforts of many different people. We do not understand that these shifts will eventually converge so that we make a quantum leap.

We create our lives through our decisions. The wry comment that "we need to be very careful what we want because we may get it" is a reminder of our capacity to change the direction of our lives. But we do need to make those decisions.

In the late seventies, my wife and I thought a great deal about whether I should continue to act as a social entrepreneur. We decided to do what was needed so I could continue in this path. As a result, I have had all the opportunities and challenges that I have wanted. On the days when they temporarily seem too much, I remind myself that I set up these conditions for myself and should not be frustrated by them!

As social entrepreneurs we have to be aware of both the world around us and our capacity to affect it. Some people are so overwhelmed by negative dynamics that they give in and cease to act. Others are so committed to Pollyanna optimism that they take on tasks that cannot be achieved regardless of the level of commitment. Effective planning for personal and social change requires realistic hope, rather than the ignoring of critical obstacles.

An enormous amount of energy is wasted these days in argument between those who are pessimistic about the future and those who are optimistic. In fact, any mature person must realize that the future is, as always, a race between education and disaster, and that the cup is always half full *and* half empty. The only new element is the fact that disaster can now be global and total, and the extent of the necessary learning is therefore far greater.

We can only deal with today's crises if we change ourselves and the society in which we live. But we cannot be effective change agents unless our statements and actions mesh. We cannot tell others to do what we say, rather than what we do. It is not enough only to change our personal styles; we must also challenge our society to alter its work, income, health, justice, and governance patterns so that rights and responsibilities are balanced realistically.   OOO

Commitments for the Twenty-First Century

Change in positive directions requires that the human race achieve an understanding of what it wants in the future. The biblical statement that "without vision the people perish" remains as true today as it has ever been in the past. John Maynard Keynes, the great British economist, made the same point when he stated: "It is ideas and not men which rule the world."

Recent successes of style over substance have caused many politicians to deny this reality. The current search in many countries is for the candidate with the right set of qualities for the TV screen: X is regarded as too cool and Y as too hot; Z is not photogenic and A has no charisma. They forget that each period has its own needs and requires a relevant spokesman. The fact that President Reagan has been widely supported in the eighties does not mean that a Reagan clone can or should be found for the nineties.

Instead, we need to set up a new set of fundamental concepts which will determine our directions. Those that follow seem to be the minimum which are necessary for the long-run survival of Planet Earth. I am particularly anxious to get feedback on this list because they are the "musts" around which I am organizing my thinking at the current time.

1. *Involuntary poverty is intolerable in the rich countries of the world.* We need to discover ways to ensure that people can obtain enough resources to live in dignity. This challenge can no longer be solved through the availability of conventional jobs for all. Fundamentally new work structures will be required. This is urgent because many of the safety-net measures which were developed in the rich countries in post-World War II years have been dismantled. Those that remain are often ineffective and counterproductive.

2. *Starvation and extreme malnutrition are intolerable anywhere in the world given our technology and our knowledge.* We must reject the proposal that some countries be permitted to collapse, not only because of our moral beliefs but also because of the dangers to our global order if our world remains divided between the haves and the have-nots. When we have eliminated starvation, then we can move against poverty on a worldwide scale. As we do so, we may discover that current food gluts will vanish and we shall once again be struggling to provide enough agricultural production to meet demands.

Eliminating starvation is unlikely without a primary commitment to population control. Failure to accept this reality will eventually lead to the draconian, dictatorial approaches to birth control which have already been taken in China and in Singapore. In addition, effective steps to feed the hungry will require the development of sustainable agriculture in the poor countries. When food aid is required, we must be far more careful about its secondary impacts.

3. *We must preserve our land and renewable resources so that our ecosystem can be maintained for the very long-term future.* The current period of surplus provides us with an extraordinary opportunity which will be lost if we continue to think in primarily economic terms. It is surely extraordinary that policy makers are considering reducing commitments to soil conservation at this moment in history when we could undo some of the losses caused by destructive uses of the soil.

One of the major issues of the next decades is the possibility of a major shift in climate patterns which could have extraordinary implications for food and fiber production. There is more and more evidence that we shall have to control CO_2 emissions due to high energy usage if we are to avoid major climatic problems.

4. *We must change our priorities from concentrating available resources on economic growth, and move toward the questions of cultural change and the quality of life.* The most crucial issues in the world today are whether we can develop social and cultural attitudes which will ensure our survival rather than continue the drive toward maximum economic growth.

5. *We must move away from assigning blame for past errors, and try to ensure equity and justice in the light of current realities.* We are still acting as though individuals always make autonomous decisions and that they should therefore be blamed for all the mistakes they make. This is often counter-productive—take, for example, the current debt crisis, particularly in agriculture. In the seventies banks poured out money, informing farmers that they could not lose. Analysts predicted that growth and inflation would go on forever. Governments challenged farmers to plant fence-

row to fencerow. Now the argument is that farmers should have realized that all this high-powered advice was wrong.

Such a stance is both radically unfair and highly dangerous, particularly when international problems are also considered. Today's internal and external debts are so huge that they will never be repaid. If we continue to act as if they will be, we shall ensure a slump. Alternatively, we can seek new patterns which will share the negative consequences of past errors as fairly as possible.

In short, the success criteria of Western societies must change dramatically. We must move away from our current concentration on maximum incomes and find new ways to balance our economy and our society.   OOO

SECTION 2

Beyond the Rapids

The first part of this book demonstrated the need to change. The next step is to learn about socioeconomic structures for our novel conditions. Fortunately, we can already see the new success criteria for our society.

All societies must make arrangements to educate people, to get work done, to keep people healthy, to provide the necessities of life, to ensure justice, to make political decisions. The unique shape of each period of history emerges from the models used to meet these needs.

All the details of our emerging directions are not known. Neither have we worked out all the implications. But we can already perceive how our socioeconomic patterns must be very different in the near future.

We are at the point where we can state the basic models by which we shall live in our emerging era. When we create conditions suitable to our new realities, people, groups, and institutions will be able to be more effective.

Education: Learning to Learn

Throughout history, human beings have passed on the knowledge of the preceding generation to the young. This strategy has been effective up to now. Today, however, the world is changing so rapidly that young and old must learn together and must rediscover the knowledge which has been lost in our ever growing "infoglut," or information overload.

Our culture has already reacted more effectively to this challenge than many of us realize. We think about education primarily in terms of schools and colleges, but these industrial-era systems are increasingly being bypassed by different systems which are providing information in more creative ways. For example, electronic communication systems get more attention from children than their classes in most cases, and the information these media convey is often more relevant, even if it grates on the sensibilities of older generations.

We need to look at the total ecology of learning and the ways that people can learn to learn in the future. We have to recognize that the so-called educational reforms in many states have actually led to a *higher* level of drop-outs. A very large percentage of students still enter college unable to read or write well enough to have any chance of graduating. In addition, a strong pattern of racial imbalance is emerging, with Asians typically doing better than whites and placing far above Blacks and Hispanics.

Within school and college systems, the key challenge facing today's teachers is to move away from a pattern which encourages people to learn information, regurgitate it, and then forget it. Young people have discovered that they can study for a test one evening and forget what they studied the next. The degree of recall of an unpopular course a few weeks after it has finished is abysmal.

In a quiz I give at my lectures across North America, I ask my audience how many believe our educational system is preparing people for the world in which they are going to live. Very few hands are raised. People are clearly discontented with educational patterns. Many, therefore, want to return to the past—to "get back to basics." But the basics have changed. The skills that people must learn to survive in the future are quite different from those which led to success in the industrial era. Equally critical, the locus of learning is changing. Just as the school and the college took over from the church and the family in the industrial era, a further enormous shift is taking place as we enter our new world.

The industrial era was based on giving and taking orders. The schoolroom taught people to live in this hierarchical world; the interactions between teachers and students reflected the relationships between bosses and workers. To prepare for a future in which human beings will work collaboratively, we need new patterns. We must learn to learn and only a small part of this new style can be taught in the conventional classroom.

One of the new hybrids is the community college. Often a number of older people in these classrooms have as much experience—or more—than the teacher. Learning is therefore a joint process with each person contributing. In the future, society will reward students for helping others to learn, as well as for their own knowledge. We may see churches and other voluntary groups pioneering these cooperative types of education. We shall also see businesses which communicate needed skills more efficiently. Information and knowledge utilities will develop which tailor responses to the need of the inquirer.

What are the vital skills of our new era? Students need to learn three *communication abilities*. The first is how to create a sense of belonging in a group—whether the group is short-term or long-term. Thought and action can only be carried out with a sense of mutual trust and commitment. Groups and organizations must have this sense of shared purpose if they are to be effective.

The second ability takes an unstructured set of realities and makes sense of them. This process is far more critical in today's world of rapid change than in the past. Fewer and fewer situations are cut and dried now. So increasingly unfamiliar conditions will require the skill of thinking through to a new understanding which enables effective action.

The third ability supports people as they work together to carry out specific actions. Good ideas are all too often spoiled by sloppy execution. The feedback of other group members to an action plan shows what is going right or wrong. These reactions to directions permit refinement of the group's perceptions and forward movement to more appropriate projects.

Within a group, each member will inevitably be better at one of these three styles than others. But some understanding of all three is necessary so that each person can appreciate the various facets of leadership.

In addition to these three communication abilities, people need to learn as many languages as they can. When we think about "languages," we usually consider French, Spanish, German, Russian, and Hopi. Each of these ways of structuring reality provides a unique window on the world. For example, people are different when they are speaking English or Hopi. Their view of the world is changed by the potentials and limitations of the language they are using. These constraints on expression can be very strong; for example, Hopi only has a present tense.

We have other "languages," however. A physics teacher once told me, "I don't try to teach my high school students physics. I show them why it is interesting to look at the world through the "language of physics." In effect, physics, chemistry, dance, anthropology, art, and computer sciences are all languages which enable us to perceive more of the world.

The more "languages" we know, the less likely we will fail to see the key reality in a situation. The broader our perception, the more effectively we shall act.

There is no limit to the process of learning to learn. Indeed, once human beings have been bitten by the excitement of finding new ways to structure knowledge, they will never again fear being bored.   OOO

The New Life Cycle

Today, the industrial-era life cycle is still seen as the norm. We expect people to go to school from the age of six to at least 16 and preferably 18, with kindergarten before and, for many, college afterwards. We expect the brightest and best to continue on to graduate school.

We still think of the average working life as being from ages 16 or 18 to 65, although people who go to college are expected to enter the labor force at a later date. We believe that most people over 65 will be retired and will get their income from social security or pensions.

Patterns in the agricultural era were very different. The life-span was much shorter—less than half the norm today. The young were expected to do agricultural work at a very early age and gained most of their education through their work.

Just as the life cycle in the industrial era was different from the agricultural, emerging era styles will also vary drastically from what came before. In fact, patterns have *already* shifted dramatically. More and more males are leaving the workforce between the ages of 55 and 65. Some of them choose to leave early. Others leave through "voluntary" early retirement programs. The employers give these workers the option of leaving early with additional retirement benefits, but the threat that they may be fired if they stay on usually exists, as well

While many older men have been leaving the labor force, the number of women of all ages in the workplace has increased extraordinarily. In the sixties, many women sought jobs to achieve meaning and autonomy in their lives. In recent years, however, more and more women have entered the labor force from necessity. Many families need two incomes to pay expenses, and many others are run solely by women.

Money pressures have, in turn, significantly reduced the number of children per family. The stereotype of the fifties family, which consisted of a man, a woman and two children, has long been outdated. For instance, many couples are choosing to remain childless. More families use sterilization than any other form of birth control. In addition, many women are bearing their children far later, having their first child between ages 30 and 40 rather than between 20 and 30. At the other end of the spectrum, many teenage women are choosing to have children in and out of wedlock and keeping them even if they are not married.

As the number of hours of work required on the job continues to decline because of the availability of computers and computer-aided machinery, far more dramatic shifts will take place. We can make them positive only if we directly face the question, how can the declining need for labor enrich rather than damage lives? We already have, in effect, a reverse leisure society, where those most financially capable of enjoying time for themselves don't have any. At the other end of the scale, those with the least skills are unemployed and find time hanging heavy on their hands. This problem will increase traumatically in the future unless we change our educational and work patterns.

Those who are concerned about unemployment often concentrate attention on the potential for further declines in the length of the work week. People point to the remarkable fact that there was a steady decline in weekly hours of work until World War II, but there has been little significant decrease in the last forty years. They suggest that the way to deal with unemployment will be to cut weekly hours of work further.

This approach fails to reflect the profound impact of the computer and advanced machinery on the type of work available. Computers will take over most of the repetitive toil in the future. The remaining human work will be increasingly demanding and require higher levels of concentration and skill from the workers.

Two key changes in our life cycle are required. The first shift will emerge as society realizes that extremely busy people cannot continue to be effective for unlimited periods of time. They inevitably suffer from burnout and cannot keep up with their field. In the future, people will be active for five, six, or seven years at a time, followed by a significant period for rest and re-creation. Even today, the demand for sabbaticals is moving beyond the educational establishment. For example, friends of mine who run a nonprofit organization recently enabled their board to see the necessity for them to get away and renew themselves for six months.

Sabbaticals will allow learning to be a lifelong process, because learning takes place in every meaningful interaction with other human beings and with the environment. One image of the new era will be the perpetual learner who develops creative capacities. We shall realize that curiosity keeps us young.

The second key change in thinking will ensure that families which choose to have children will be given time and resources to raise them well. More creative educational patterns are only feasible when parents are able to nurture their children. Many young people fail to cope with a rapidly changing world primarily because both parents were overloaded by their jobs or there is a single parent trying to raise children alone. Fortunately new child-rearing systems are emerging based on extended families linked by blood or joint concerns.

We are raising many children who are almost inevitably doomed to be locked out of the functioning society—in America, estimates range from 15 percent and up. Percentages may be even higher in Europe where jobs are scarce and unemployment has beccome a way of life. These young people currently have no prospect of grasping the complexities of our knowledge-based universe. We can no longer tolerate a society in which more and more children have less and less psychic and practical support.   OOO

Redefining Work

There was no split between the concepts of work and leisure in hunting and gathering or agricultural societies. The industrial era created, and continues to reinforce strongly, the belief that your job can be cut off from the rest of your life. In the emerging era, we need to return to the sense that work is an integral part of one's life—though not the whole of it.

In the mid-1800s, a typical man would spend 40 percent of his life on the job. Today this figure is down to 14 percent. Part of this extraordinary change results from a decrease in the average work week from 70 or even 80 hours to 40 or fewer. In addition, people are now far older when they enter the labor force and live longer after retirement. Lengthened vacations and paid holidays make the ratio of work time to non-work time even lower.

Despite the decline in life-time hours of work, unemployment and underemployment rates have grown to the double-digit range in many Western countries—and may amount to a third or even a half of the labor force, in the poor countries. We need to reexamine how we should structure work in the light of our rapidly changing realities.

Our culture currently sends profoundly mixed messages about the attractiveness of work and jobs. I first really "saw" the cultural assumption that jobs should be unpleasant when I was working with a psychologist in the early sixties. We had been talking about the need for rethinking patterns of activity and their rewards. Despite this discussion, the psychologist remarked at the end of a week's activity that he had enjoyed himself so much that he really should not be paid! Many of us still internalize the biblical view that work is a curse. It follows that enjoying work is almost immoral!

Should we imagine and create a world where most of the work is done by people who like what they are doing? Can we develop a society where people enjoy their activities while the unpleasant chores are fairly allocated among all workers? The increasing competence of machines makes these questions not only meaningful but crucial.

Reactions to the feasibility of the positive changes these questions suggest is determined largely by our beliefs about the nature of human beings. Do we believe deep down that most people are idle and irresponsible and have to be forced into activity? Or are we convinced that healthy human beings want to grow and help others to grow?

I work out of the second assumption, having seen much evidence of its validity and knowing that it is the requirement for our survival. We need approaches which enable people to be as effective as they can so their competencies increase. We can then deal with those individuals who do not accept the challenge: experience shows that only a few reject opportunities to expand their potential.

Some people fear that there will not be enough work to do in the future. On the contrary, anybody who has learned to learn is always trying to find time to accomplish even a small portion of what is possible and interesting. We need more people in education, in the care of the young and the old, in support of the environment, in the arts, and in social entrepreneurship. We need to help each other find out where we can grow and develop the potential which exists in each one of us. We need to help each other discover creative directions. Most importantly, we need to end the sharp division between work and leisure.

The current worldwide shortage of "jobs" will inevitably worsen. If we choose to remain wedded to the concept of full employment in its current form, the degree of stress within and between countries will increase dramatically. We must therefore move beyond the models which have worked well in the industrial era. We must commit to making meaningful activity and the opportunity to earn resources available to all citizens. We must end the current split where some are bored because they have nothing worthwhile to do, while others are overstressed because they never catch up with their responsibilities.

Unfortunately, discussions of desirable work patterns are blocked in Western society because of the tight linkage between work, income, and dignity. Discussions of how we could do the needed work differently almost always bog down because of the implicit or explicit question, "But how will people earn their living?" or the statement, "Everybody ought to have a job."

In the future, we are not only going to need new ways of thinking about work, but also new ways in which to develop and share resources. Limits to production will not be set in the future by the productive capacity of machines, but by the need to avoid stressing the environment excessively. We must not fall into the trap of believing that current short-run patterns of excess energy, food, and raw materials imply that there are no long-run constraints on production.

Work patterns are central to the fabric of any culture. This issue is critically important to more and more people, particularly for the growing number of people who want autonomy and responsibility in their work and also time for a personal life.   OOO

Distributive Justice

Current patterns of income distribution are often seen as sacred. It is widely argued that nobody should make proposals which change the amount of money that individuals earn or keep after taxes. This argument is still heard despite the fact that tax laws and discriminatory government policies have been shifting rights to income and wealth throughout the twentieth century.

The belief that people's earnings should not be affected by taxes is based on the argument that income is equal to economic contribution. This assertion is attributed to the pioneering economist Adam Smith, who is widely believed to have argued that any interference in free market activities would inevitably damage society. In reality, Smith accepted considerable government intervention as necessary.

Arguments for not interfering in income distribution patterns are also based on the ideas of a group of late nineteenth century economists who "proved" that everybody gets paid what they are worth *so long as free market conditions exist*. Unfortunately, we almost always ignore the corollary that without free markets the distribution of income is not based on economics but politics.

Free markets require that all businesses be small, information moves perfectly, governments not intervene, and there be no labor unions. These conditions are, of course, not realized today. Incomes therefore depend, in large part, on power and influence. Big businesses, government, and unions all distort rewards and information to benefit themselves. Consequently, both our internal and international economic systems lead to profound social injustice.

A further critical assumption lies behind all current discussions of the distribution of income. Work is defined as something that people do not want to do and money as the reward that compensates for the unpleasantness of work. Suppose, however, that jobs continue to be scarce. What would reward structures look like in such dramatically changed conditions?

Monetary rewards are still generally assumed to be the best way to motivate people to work harder. The growing gap between the rich and the poor, both within countries and between them, is presented as an efficient way to create greater drive. Extreme differentials in wealth are justified as a means to ensure that there will be fewer poor people in the next generation. For instance, a 1986 column by William Safire in the New York Times proposed that we should remove greed from the list of the seven deadly sins. He argued that the drive of the motivated few, with consequent monetary rewards, is the only way to care for the needs of the masses.

Economic entrepreneurship alone will not create social justice, however. The individual's effort to maximize his own wealth, largely regardless of secondary consequences, served the society in the past because it increased production with limited negative results. In today's conditions, with decreasing amounts of easily available energy and raw materials, as well as dangers of abusing the environment beyond the point of no return, we must find ways to do more with less.

Despite the economic recovery of 1983-1986, the U.S. Conference of Mayors reported that there was a significant increase in demands for emergency food, shelter, and economic assistance during the winters of this recovery. As a consequence, church aid, which was originally meant to be available for emergencies only, is now integrated into welfare systems.

Hodding Carter summed up his distress about current trends in a 1986 *Wall Street Journal* column entitled "A Have and Have-Not America." He wrote, "Even as the evidence grows steadily stronger that we are building a class-ridden society of ever-sharper contrasts between haves and have-nots, we are treated to long treatises on the triumph of capitalism and the American dream...The problem is that we are structuring a country in which Third World conditions exist side-by-side with prosperity. It is...social dynamite."

In July 1986, the San Francisco Director of Planning was assaulted by one of the homeless created by the process of office building and gentrification in the city. This experience could have reminded the city staff of the need to deal with extreme poverty. Instead, the city merely reinforced police patrols in the area around the director's office so that the evidence of societal breakdown would be removed from view.

Disraeli, a great British prime minister, once said that Britain could not long survive half rich and half poor. His message is just as relevant today, both nationally and internationally. We have little time to avoid the profound dangers which will emerge if we perpetuate the ever-growing chasm between those with great wealth and those suffering from grinding poverty.

The worsening problems resulting from the mal-distribution of income is a symptom of the growing chasm between those who can find and use information and knowledge and those who cannot. Poverty will not be resolved without dealing with this critical broader issue.   OOO

Citizenship

America's overwhelming commitment to economic growth, which emerged during the Great Depression, has devalued the importance of citizenship. We have acted as though economists could and should determine the general good. This was the implication of the famous statement, "What is good for General Motors is good for America."

The extent of the shift is illustrated by Willis Harman, president of the *Institute of Noetic Sciences* and a well-known futurist. He tells audiences that his grandmother would have been horrified if she had been described as a "consumer." She was a citizen and she knew it. Her respect went to those who observed the responsibilities of citizenship. Many younger people also reject our stress on the importance of material goods.

We can only break out of the drive toward consumerism, however, when we recognize how and why it is built into our current system. More goods and services are produced each year as firms become more efficient and more productive. At first sight, this increased production seems highly valuable. There are apparently many positive options. People, especially poorer individuals, can consume more goods that are actually needed. Or individuals can take time off; after all, unemployment is only misallocated free time! Or society can provide resources to those in need; certainly nobody would deny the extent of deprivation in the world.

Our central dilemma is that choosing any *positive* direction for using additional goods depends on *political* decisions. In the absence of creative actions, societies are trapped within a whirling dervish economy dependent on compulsive consumption. The current system depends on people wanting more than they can afford and buying it despite their lack of resources. More and more people are dissatisfied with this way of living but an effective challenge cannot be mounted until we move out of our industrial-era systems.

Many historians argue that cultures move through a series of phases and that trying to change these phases is like hoping to hold back the tides. Challenging citizens to live responsible lives after a society has emphasized softness and wealth seems impossible to these analysts. They may be right. There is, however, one certainty in life: if we decide that something is impossible, it certainly won't be accomplished!

Why might our society decide to accept the challenge of citizenship? Much evidence demonstrates that more and more people want to be effectively involved in making decisions about their own lives. As I travel in America and Britain, I discover that many communities have begun to revitalize themselves and to ask hard questions about what is worthwhile. Polls show that many people are as interested in enhancing their quality of life as in increasing the quantity of goods they purchase and consume.

For instance, Iowans concerned about the future recently collected over 100 case studies about positive efforts to improve the quality of life being made in the state. Not all of them will be successful, of course. There is, nevertheless, great ferment generating exciting new ideas. Similar studies in Europe also show creativity in communities.

These emerging ideas are still not really visible to the mainstream, however. Our current problem is similar to the difficulties which occur when theories are challenged in the physical sciences. Individual scientists, and the groups within which they are organized, resist new ideas because they threaten current understandings and prestige patterns. Change can only occur when the breakdown of the old becomes truly obvious and the vision of the new becomes clear.

A shift often appears to be incredibly rapid and overwhelming to those who become aware of the new patterns at a late date. They have no idea of the amount of time which went into the preparatory work. Actually, just as few successes develop in the life of individuals without preparation and effort, shifts in worldviews are never created rapidly. Nor do they develop without political effort. All of us must be involved in the hard process of helping people think about issues of equity and governance.

People need to accept their citizenship responsibilities so that new options can be developed for a new era. Unfortunately, industrial-era cultures provide few rewards to citizens and offer more brickbats than goodies to those who enter social change and governmental roles. I once knew a woman who was encouraged by many friends and colleagues to run for mayor. She won. The day after the election she was asked why she was on the take! This is an extreme example but a telling one.

In contrast, citizenship was the ideal in Athens at the time of its highest civilization. Every non-slave male was challenged to aspire to proficiency as a speaker and persuader. Will we develop a parallel goal for all members of our society in time to prevent developing breakdowns? Will we provide psychic and pragmatic rewards to those who commit energy to governance issues?

The major shifts we require are impossible until we decide to challenge current patterns of thought and behavior. But renewal can be achieved if we return to some of our most fundamental traditions. The first step is for each of us to decide that we have a personal responsibility for the society in which we live. The second is to accept that there are no pat answers, but that each of us must struggle to apply the values of faith, honesty, responsibility, humility, and love to real-life situations without prejudgment.   OOO

Promotive Health

One of the most encouraging aspects of the current scene is the extraordinary change in perceptions of medical and health issues. In the early seventies, my wife and I were involved with a small group of people in Hawaii who started a health network. It aimed to make people aware of their capacity to look after their bodies and minds and challenged existing medical and psychiatric models.

At the time, most people felt that our group was tilting at windmills. North Americans, they argued vehemently, would never be willing to look after themselves—they would go on expecting doctors to make their decisions for them. Today, some fifteen years later, this prediction has proved radically false. The amount of time, effort, and money spent to promote health throughout the world is very significant and still rising. The emerging model for health care is people cooperating to keep themselves healthy and medical costs as low as possible.

There is growing understanding that diet, sensible exercise, good sleeping patterns, and avoidance of excess in all fields can improve health and increase longevity. I saw how far the change had come when I talked in 1986 to the leaders of three Catholic hospital groups which had merged. I was excited to discover that some of them could see how a promotive health orientation could help patients and families to heal themselves, and also be profitable for the hospital. They perceived an opportunity to return to their human-care roots rather than be caught up in an efficient high-tech orientation, where the patient is an object to be manipulated rather than a person to be supported.

The drive toward promotive health became visible nationally when the costs of medical care in America rose above 10 percent of the gross national product in the early 1980s. There is now a recognition, not only in America but throughout the world, that medical costs cannot continue to rise as a percentage of total available resources. But this realization alone could not keep medical costs from increasing at triple the rate of the general inflation index in as late as mid-1986.

In order to reverse this trend, hospitals, insurance systems, and self-care groups are emphasizing the need for people to look after themselves. At first sight, this change appears to be almost pure gain. Surely it is better to challenge people to keep themselves healthy than to permit themselves to get sick. Realistically, however, all changes bring both benefits and costs.

Even if people commit to health strategies, there will not be enough medical care to go around. If we choose to keep people alive by extraordinary technological means, less care will be available for poorer people. This dilemma has already become acute.

Obviously, we shall have to ration medical care; the only question is how. We must start, of course, from the recognition that there is no perfect rationing mechanism. Indeed, significant differences in approach are already appearing even in Western societies, and not all work as planned. For example, the National Health Service in Britain aimed to eliminate the impact of wealth on health care. But favorable treatment for the wealthy has crept back in, both through the growth of private health systems and because doctors typically give better care to people they like than to those outside their social class. Much of the initial commitment does remain, however.

In the United States, quality of care is openly tied to ability to pay. In theory, those who are truly poor are cared for, but the safety net has developed many holes in recent years. Poor patients are all too frequently denied entrance to hospitals, and scandals erupt with increasing frequency when they die before they can get care elsewhere. In addition, a growing number of people are not eligible for support under poverty programs, but cannot afford medical insurance. This problem is a time bomb waiting to explode!

Another critical future issue will be the right/responsibility of the society to prevent behavior which increases the danger of ill health or accident. This pressure has led to increased limits on choice. A growing number of countries now require helmets for motorcycle riders. Many states have seat-belt laws. There are developing demands to limit smoking because of health risks and the costs they impose on the society. Obesity is also being discouraged because of its contribution to ill health.

Soon those who are believed to have contributed to their illnesses by their life-style may be required to pay more for medical care. This pattern already exists to a limited extent where higher insurance rates are required for bad risks like smokers. The tough question society must ask is, "When does intelligent support of healthful behavior shade over into the destruction of freedom?" This issue is frequently raised and over-ridden, for example, when seat-belt legislation is considered.

Societies are, in reality, already rationing health care; difficulties will increase dramatically as the population ages.

So long as industrial-era thought patterns dominate, the tension will be between the following two models:

• Care will be made available to those who can pay and those without money will be treated less well. This will benefit the rich as against the poor; *or*

• Care will be provided to those who have the best statistical chance of survival. A primary problem with this approach is that statistics are meaningless when applied to individuals.

Neither of these approaches faces the depth of our challenges. We must struggle with the moral and ethical issues which have emerged as medicine keeps us alive beyond our natural life span. And we must also struggle with the questions of who pays for health care, and to what extent society has the right to limit the options of its citizens "for their own good."   OOO

Justice

In every society, some people will try to take advantage of others. Justice systems are designed to minimize the damage caused by self-centered and destructive behavior.

There is a wide range of patterns in justice systems throughout the world. Some Arabic countries inherit traditional Islamic law, which is based on rapid, visible punishment. The belief is that quick and violent retaliation will prevent others from acting in similar ways. Western countries see Islamic styles of punishment as barbaric, but often forget that our system of imprisonment also has its problems. Prisons are deeply destructive of human dignity and potential and create hardened criminals, as the recent investigation of the Texas system has shown.

In almost all areas of the world, legal systems tend to support the powerful and concentrate punishment on the poor. In the Western world, the rich and the powerful have learned to use all available loopholes. Even when convicted, they benefit from the odd belief that "they have suffered enough," and receive lighter sentences. The underprivileged are far more likely to be convicted; their poverty is not seen as an excuse for crime.

Many examinations have shown the weaknesses of the current Western criminal-justice system. But we still are not undertaking a *systemic* analysis of our system. Jails necessarily brutalize both criminals and warders. This was brilliantly demonstrated in a Stanford University experiment which confined college students. Full-scale guard/prisoner pathologies were created in less than a week.

We also need to recognize the police/criminal/courts sub-culture and the way that it adapts to the overloads which society has placed upon it. Interestingly, such television shows as *Hill Street Blues*, *LA Law*, and *Cagney and Lacey* give a better sense of these systemic issues than do most academic treatises.

Once we recognize that we face an overall problem, we will stop hoping to find solutions by improving one part of the system, for example, by concentrating on the performance of the police or the courts. We cannot hope to make any real progress until we decide what our goals should be. How can we effectively decrease self-destruction and social damage?

In the past, societies with a single set of rules and behavior patterns accepted by the vast majority of their members have limited crime most efficiently. Under these circumstances, most people accept dominant cultural patterns, and those who do not are largely controlled by their peers. This pattern of conformity was the rule in many tribes and in small towns. The approach was effective, but the cost in lost creativity cannot be accepted in today's world.

Given the inevitability of human diversity in the future, we must not expect people to live by a single set of rules.

Indeed, it has become impossible to create laws which will serve the needs of all people. Rather, people and groups must learn to behave appropriately, given their own sense of what is required on the basis of their spiritual values. They must also learn to respect the different patterns chosen by others.

Human survival now depends on the development of a sense of personal responsibility. Instead of relying primarily on the police and the courts to enforce conformity, societies will depend on human beings acting as seems appropriate to them within their unique, positive-value perceptions.

What specific pragmatic implications does this have for shifts in systems now?

First, we need to recreate a sense of personal discipline in such minor matters as obeying traffic lights and other social norms which are devised for our safety. One of the frightening social breakdowns in recent years has been the number of people who run traffic lights and stop signs unless the police are around to penalize them.

Second, a great deal of the over-regulation in our societies could be eliminated if groups were prepared to discipline their own members. It is obvious that many of the current constraints on various professions and businesses developed because they were unwilling to control themselves. Courts and outside disciplinary boards have been relied upon because peers have been unwilling to face the unpleasant reality of rotten apples in every barrel. The excessive costs of insurance and litigation can only be reduced when professions act to preserve their own standards.

Third, and most critically, we have to undercut the criminal culture. We need to find ways to prevent people from entering the criminal class, recognizing that young people may well be trapped for life once they are touched by it. Sending a youth to reform school or jail all too often creates a repeat offender rather than ensuring rehabilitation. The primary purpose of an effective justice system should be to protect the society rather than punish the offender.

One first step in breaking out of our current dilemmas is to look honestly at the drug issue. From the point of view of the drug dealer, the governments of the world are in the business of creating an artificial scarcity which maximizes profits. So long as this policy continues, the illegal drug business generates enough money to corrupt all but the most honest. The cold fact is that people cannot be prevented from destroying their lives. We have accepted this reality for cigarette smokers and drinkers. Our only hope is to extend this recognition to drugs, and, *at the same time*, commit to deglamorizing *all* self-destructive behavioral habits while providing opportunities for those who commit to healing themselves.

A just society would undercut most of the sources of crime. We should then be able to deal with the minority who have a pathological need to hurt and destroy others.

OOO

Creating a High Quality of Life

John Cage, the avant-garde composer, said many years ago, "Measurements measure measuring means." This cryptic statement implies that *what* we choose to measure is more important than the findings from our measurements. Western societies today concentrate on economic factors. We do not measure the *quality* of our individual or our community lives.

Our emerging era will be based on different measurements; indeed the Western passion for measurement will *itself* decrease in the future. But measurement is still one of the ways that Western people learn about reality most easily. We must find different ways of satisfying the need for figures and data.

People often assume that the "gross national product" measures not only economic but also social satisfaction. GNP, however, counts only those activities which are carried out for money. So when a person moves out of the monetary into the non-monetary sector, previously measured work is ignored.

This point became clear to me one day when I was painting the fence in front of our house. I suddenly realized that my work was not being counted as part of national production—a true insult to an economist!

The gross national product would therefore be highest if *all* activity was carried out for money and no exchanges were motivated by family ties, friendship, or volunteer effort. Few people, even few economists, would be enthusiastic about a society which was structured along these lines.

The second problem with using GNP to measure human satisfaction is that it makes no distinction between "goods" and "bads." The money spent to have an enjoyable vacation is part of the GNP, but so is the money you spend to burglar-proof your house. I once garnered a risky headline in a heart-land paper when I was quoted, correctly, as having stated that burning down the state capitol and having to rebuild it would be good for the GNP.

One obvious direction in which we can move is to find ways to determine the quality of life. Many groups have tried to do this, but they have failed in two critical areas. First, they have argued that the quality of life is an objective measure which can be determined on the basis of criteria created by experts. This denies the diversity in the world.

The second problem is related to the first. Most survey-ing services have published their lists with a ranking from top to bottom in terms of attractiveness, assuming that the factors affecting the quality of life are the same in cities and small communities. Recently, Rand McNally created so much anger in the town listed last in liveability that there was a ceremonial burning of Rand McNally atlases.

Having lived in a number of countries including India, France, Scotland, and the United States, I am very well aware that what is important to people in one nation may be far less critical to citizens of another part of the world. A feeling of quality is profoundly subjective.

Any useful quality of life survey must therefore start from the assumption that each community is unique and its needs can only be discovered in terms of local conditions. This means that qualities of life cannot be compared between communities but can only be described in terms of success or failure in meeting the community's own goals. Communities will also change their goals and their priorities from year to year.

How can we develop a quality of life survey? The first step would be to determine what is most important to citizens. The easiest way to accomplish this might be to ask a random grouping of citizens what elements in the life of the community they valued most. Surveyors should take care to keep questions open-ended and to include people from all parts of the community.

From this survey, investigators would establish a list. Citizens would be given 100 votes or $100 and asked to allocate them among various quality of life elements. Confronted with this opportunity, respondents would not have to choose a single critical issue. Very few people would be willing to spend all of their votes or dollars on one problem or priority, so a spectrum of issues would emerge.

This survey would give members of town and city councils evidence of what is truly important to their constituents. Currently, political officers do not know what citizens *really* want. This initial survey would provide them basic information. The pattern of knowledge could be enhanced by some fairly simple computer programs, which would make clear how patterns of thinking varied by neighborhood within larger communities.

This survey could be repeated at intervals to provide updated information about attitudes. With a series of surveys, officeholders would discover if people feel that the quality of life was getting better or worse. The next step would be to set up a process where people could provide their input to the city council any time they wished, using existing computer hardware and programming. This model could later develop into a feedback process between the decision-makers of the community and its citizens.

One of the most exciting consequences of this whole effort would be to break the stranglehold so often held by special interest groups. At the current time, it is difficult to tell if the small group that comes to community meetings on specific subjects is just a fringe group or represents a larger constituency. The availability of a citizen polling device would show if the issue was important to a significant number of people or just to a vocal few.

One of the most urgent requirements in communities is to ensure that decision-making meets the needs of most citizens rather than its strident minorities. A quality of life index could help ensure this result and is one place to start changing our political patterns.   OOO

The Compassionate Era

We are moving out of the industrial era into a profoundly new period of history. This period has been given many names: the era of relationships, the planetary era, the compassionate era.

Many provocative phrases have been developed to help us glimpse part of the universe growing around us. People argue the need for "all-win, cooperative systems"; this approach is advanced by such groups as *Common Ground* and *Action Linkage*. People talk about the development of a "better game than war" which can seize our energies and our loyalties; this approach is advanced by *Earthstewards, Beyond War*, and the *Institute of Noetic Sciences*.

Can we sense a new holy grail? Can we discover a single vision that will inspire us? I doubt that there will be a clear, exciting, *unique* image. In a world where there are no certainties—except the certainty of uncertainty—we must learn to live for the smaller joys, the simpler pleasures, and the more manageable challenges. We are rediscovering how to survive pain and grief, so we can savor love and joy.

In the future, we shall measure our lives by our own growth and our ability to help others to grow. I remember Gregory Bateson, one of the most provocative thinkers of our time, reminiscing about a colleague who was reaching the end of his life. This dying man valued the education which had enabled his students to be effective and imaginative. He was particularly excited because they were not clones of himself but had all found their own unique niches.

In the past, we have seen our children as the way to ensure immortality. So people have been frustrated when their families died out. In the future we shall understand that we gain immortality through the ideas we have passed on to others and which they, in turn, have internalized and made their own. We shall be excited, rather than threatened, when people surpass our skills, because they can then teach us directly and save us time and effort.

This is one critical example of the developing change in our success criteria. In today's world, where everyone must earn a living in a world of high unemployment, we are inevitably threatened when people become more expert than we are. But in our emerging relational universe, we shall be pleased to find people who can speed and clarify our learning process.

We will not achieve Utopia or perfection, however. In many ways, conflict will increase as we accept that it is inevitable and healthy. We shall learn to use *conflict* as a spur to *creativity* rather than as a justification for violence. In the future, the clash of experience and perceptions will uncover the potentials for new understandings which are stored in these differences.

Of course, our future directions may appear intolerably woolly and vague to goal-oriented people with industrial-era values. The MBA-trained management student has little understanding of, or tolerance for, the complexities and paradoxes of leadership activities. The human relationships vital to effective leadership can easily be dismissed as "warm fuzzies."

We are now at the heart of our current dilemmas. The emerging wisdom of our new period is largely invisible to those who believe in industrial-era styles. Compassion in the industrial era is often equated with weakness. But in the future, we must see it as our greatest strength. We must relearn the skill of "walking a mile in another's moccasins." We need to feel "passion with"—this is the literal translation of compassion.

Fortunately, we do not have to invent the wisdom we need. It is available in the world's oldest and deepest spiritual traditions. It can also be found in the newest understandings of system theory and leadership. Each person's approach will depend on the journey taken but we shall all draw from the same deep well.

The compassionate era will transform the industrial era totally. The change will be even more thorough and complete than the shift from the agricultural era to the industrial era, and far more sudden. If we look back at the works of the great nineteenth-century novelists like Dickens, we can see the generational clash between points of view in that earlier shift. Today, we cannot wait for the carriers of the old culture to die; all of us have to rethink how we see the world during our lifetimes.

We can think of ourselves as undergoing a "mind-quake." Mind-quakes occur when an old dominant way of thinking is overridden by undeniable new understandings. We must jointly create a new era which recognizes the inevitability of uncertainty and values honesty, responsibility, humility, faith, and love as survival skills.

We must learn to live with the quietness of process rather than the franticness of goals. We shall enjoy the challenges of cooperation rather than the discords of competition. We shall support the complexities of diversity and reject the blandness of over-ordered efficiencies.

Those of us who travel have watched as airports are built and rebuilt while the flights go on. We must also learn how to change systems while they continue to operate on the societal scale.

We are creating a very different world. As we begin to discover its style, we shall like ourselves better, learn to use our strengths, and manage our weaknesses. Above all, we shall know that we can achieve nothing significant without colleagues who share our fundamental hopes and dreams and help us develop them. We shall show that this new world can develop more positive energy with less cost than the industrial era it is already replacing.   OOO

SECTION 3

Leadership Patterns in the Rapids

Individual and social behavior will only change if we provide opportunities for discussion and link people who can help each other. We must set out knowledge in more accessible and less contradictory ways.

These three tasks all require alterations in our styles of leadership. We need to work with each other rather than be controlled by hierarchical authority.

In the future the right to lead will be based on competence and knowledge rather than position. This will challenge the bureaucratic styles which currently dominate most of our decision-making.

The material in this section deals with new understandings of leadership and followership. The new styles of leadership create higher levels of effectiveness in dealing with the discontinuities of the future.

Power and Authority

Many years ago, at the end of an intensive three-day seminar, a nun said to me, "I think I've finally learned what you've been saying. You are asking each of us to be our own hero or heroine." I've used her insight many times in recent years.

Histories published today usually emphasize the great human being. One person, usually male, is seen as creating extraordinary changes in the culture and society. We concentrate on that person's behavior and how history changed to fit the leader's values and desired directions.

This view follows from certain theories about power. We use a top-down model of decision-making which can be traced to many traditional theologies. "God is all knowing. What happens in the world should therefore not be challenged." This view is still dominant in the structures of many of the religions of the world and in some Christian denominations.

In the Christian church, God's authority was delegated first to popes and then to kings. The pope could make statements with the authority of God. Kings also held power from God, through the pope; to challenge the king's authority was treasonous.

In the twentieth century, this top-down type of power is used by most organizations. These hierarchies are still based on the belief that *anybody* at the top has the right to be in control and to give orders. Instructions, whether they make sense or not, are enforced by sticks and carrots. This model applies not only in the military, but also within bureaucratic organizations of all sorts.

This leads to major problems when many different systems, all of which have power, try to force their special interest patterns on the total society. In complex situations, this often results in deadlock with each group distorting the information they put out to support their special-interest position. We see the consequent problems internationally, at national and state levels, and sometimes even within communities.

Aware of this deadlock between conflicting power groups, some people are calling for the reconcentration of power. They want to find a "benevolent" dictator, who will make the necessary decisions without the confusion created by democratic processes. This approach appears tidy and efficient at first sight. It will not work, however, because power necessarily corrupts information. The more power people wield, the less their subordinates will tell them what ought to be known for fear that their challenges will lead to negative job ratings or even being fired. In today's world of rapid change, concentration of power is counterproductive.

Others take a polar-opposite position. They propose that government should be based on the belief that everybody is *equally* informed and intelligent. This style of thinking has led in recent years to two proposals: that legislators should be chosen by lot, and also that the most important government directions should be decided by referenda.

Unfortunately, these cures would be worse than the current disease. Leadership requires commitment, a quality not found by lottery. Similarly, making important decisions on the basis of referenda assumes either that we can all be sufficiently informed about issues without studying them, or that we can all take the necessary time for study of a wide variety of issues. The first response is obviously ridiculous. The second is also infeasible because of the range of issues in the world and their complexity.

We must rediscover the stance which lies between these two extremes. Citizens must be informed so that they can choose their desired overall direction. But people who enjoy spending the time and effort necessary to study and work on critical issues must choose to do so if we are to make positive decisions.

There is a need for "servant leadership." This is not a new model, having existed throughout Western and Eastern history. It is the style Lao Tzu imagined when he observed, "When the leader leads well, the people say they did it themselves." It is the pattern of Christ who came to show the way and not to force people to follow it. It is a model being advanced by more and more business authorities.

Servant leadership is also called "sapiential authority"—it puts the right to make decisions in the hands of those who are most competent. Of course, nobody is competent at everything; we need to learn to lead where we can and follow when we should.

We learn to live well when we discover our strengths and weaknesses. We can then maximize our strengths and limit the negative effects of our weaknesses. So the good leader is one who helps groups form in ways which support each person's strengths and combine them effectively, while limiting the dangers of their weaknesses. The best leaders understand this style instinctively, a theme which runs through such naval book series as C. S. Forester's books where Hornblower is admired without his ever understanding what he is doing right for his officers and crew.

Women generally use servant leadership styles more easily than men. The required change from male-dominant styles of leadership to female "power-with" patterns will stress cultures profoundly. The cross-currents will be even fiercer than might be anticipated because many women have accepted male styles and will not easily give them up: Mrs. Thatcher, the Prime Minister of Great Britain, is an obvious example.

Servant leadership has been the maverick style in the past. So many who are otherwise fully in tune with the need for fundamental change cannot accept that it must be the dominant style of the future. Servant leadership demands that we commit ourselves to our own growth and that of others. This can only take place when we accept ourselves and our fallibilities. Balancing these two perceptions leads us to the tensions between leadership and followership.   OOO

Leadership and Followership

The primary organizational form in today's world is bureaucracy. It exists in the capitalist and the communist worlds, and now dominates the poor countries as well. It is the primary structure for businesses and governments and churches and nonprofit organizations. If bureaucracies were an appropriate way to manage today's conditions, society would be in fine shape. But, given the need for open decision-making based on rapidly changing realities, we need to organize using profoundly different principles.

There may well be as many definitions of bureaucracy as there are scholars of the subject. Its characteristics emerge from industrial-era patterns of thought. Authority is hierarchical and the right to make decisions depends on rank. Those in charge concentrate on short-run goals and decisions which will hopefully deliver positive immediate results. Subordinates who challenge actions are likely to get themselves fired. Even those whistle-blowers who try to make the system accept its *own* norms and beliefs usually lose their jobs. This leads to a lack of individual responsibility. So the primary difficulty today is institutional malfunction, rather than individual sin.

Bureaucracies are supposed to operate on clear and understandable rules, designed to avoid arbitrary treatment and to ensure equity and justice. We now realize, however, that real people don't fit tidily into defined boxes. This means that somebody always has to exercise judgment. Maintaining the pretense that bureaucrats can successfully solve all problems "by the book" downgrades both the bureaucrat and the citizen.

This reality is clearly visible in the field of taxation. The tax code has become so complex and its interpretation so difficult that tax agents inevitably reach varying conclusions. This would be true even if they only applied the tax code to the "facts." Given that they have to make choices in negotiations, the personalities of agents will inevitably affect how they apply the law. The style and practice of bureaucratic systems depend heavily on who works within them and who heads them.

Rather than trying to erase personality, we must change our institutional arrangements to reflect the impact of varying approaches. We must discover how people can work effectively with each other. This subject is the central theme of much discussion today, and has been raised in books like *Leaders* by Warren Bennis and Burt Nanus which shows the type of leadership required for today's conditions.

There is already remarkably complete agreement about the types of changes which are going to be required to build more responsive institutions. We need to encourage leadership which develops and supports desirable long-run directions within the rapids of change. There is far less certainty, however, about the processes which can help current institutions develop these new and more desirable characteristics.

As we move toward creating a value-based society, bureaucracies will inevitably be replaced by networks and linkages. These will act on the basis of competence and knowledge, with the most competent person having maximum influence on decision-making. This leader will understand the vision of the organization, as well as the various activities required to realize this vision.

In addition, an effective leader must also understand the changes taking place in the outside world which affect what will be possible and desirable. Those who manage our future institutions will need a grasp of the discontinuities being caused by weaponry, environmental realities, computers and robots, biology, climate and population shifts, as well as many other dynamics.

Heads of these future institutions will have the right to give orders, but only as long as the orders "make sense." Leaders will no longer be supported regardless of whether they are right or wrong. Instead, we must sharpen our leader-critiquing skills in ways which enhance rather than destroy systems. And we must learn how to determine whether instructions make sense.

Leaders and followers must not only know what to do, but also when they are out of their depth. People who act when they are not competent often cause the most damage. It is actually far more critical that people *ask* somebody when they don't know how to act than it is for them to be effective when they are already able to make the right decision.

When I was consulting in Nebraska, a group of state agency heads met to discuss fundamental change issues. They developed the following image. Each organization usually has two types of "fires": one is designed to keep the staff warm and happy; the other will destroy the system if it gets out of hand. The truly dangerous employee is the person who pours water on the fires which are desirable and gasoline on the dangerous conflagration!

Hierarchical structures are not effective in times of rapid change because they inevitably block information movement. We must create systems in which competence and knowledge are valued above manipulation. Fortunately, some organizations already operate in this way. We need to learn from their experience. Such institutions as *Innovation Associates* are concentrating on building these necessary skills.

Institutional renewal is possible and has been achieved in schools, colleges, churches, businesses and many other settings. But it can only take place when existing leadership is supportive, and when the organization believes in itself, recognizes that it is facing a crisis, and knows that the answers of the past are no longer adequate.   OOO

Leadership Patterns for Changing Realities

The need for leadership is a constant. But the required style of leadership changes with the times. We live in a period when there are no certainties. We are caught in the rapids of change but we have not, as yet, created the social structures appropriate either for the current transition or the compassionate era we are entering.

Are our times truly unique, or are we dramatizing the extent of our possibilities and problems compared to other periods? Often at the end of centuries, and particularly at the end of millennia, people believe that the end of the world is coming. In the late 1900s, are we caught in this same illusion?

In fact, our challenges are new for two reasons. The arguments used in the 1984 pamphlet *At the Crossroads* put out by the Communications Era Task Force are convincing. "First, [the shift] is taking place within the lifetime of those alive today.... For the first time, human beings must deliberately search for new ways to understand the world if it, and we, are to survive. Second, since the beginning of history, people have given their loyalty to their own group and feared or mistrusted outsiders. Today, our power has become so great that the violence which results from our fear can end in total destruction. We must therefore eliminate the 'we-they,' win-lose patterns which have dominated our thinking and replace them with win-win styles."

Today's challenges are truly different in style and in scope. Of course, the greatest threat arises from the implications of modern weapons. Those who want to emphasize continuity claim that throughout history, all new weapons have been seen as cataclysmic. They suggest that the nuclear bomb is only one more step in the long process of increased destructive power.

But even if one discounts the dangers of "nuclear winter"—the threat that sunshine might be prevented from reaching the earth after a nuclear exchange—the potential destructive power from using only a small proportion of current nuclear weaponry is crushing. Similarly, new chemical and biological weapons can destroy civilization. As long as war remains an accepted way of resolving disputes, we risk a holocaust which would end the globe's evolutionary development.

Some of those who recognize the true dangers of modern weapons suggest that we could get rid of them and then use war again as a method of settling disputes! Such a stance is naive, because the knowledge we have gained about today's weapons cannot be abandoned. It is also tragic, because modern weaponry can actually help the human race to grow up. Nuclear, biological, and chemical weaponry have made massive violence infeasible; the human race must learn to work together, or it will perish.

If we are to move beyond violence, we must change our personal behavior patterns as individuals. War is only one symptom of our destructive belief systems, which do not fit a world with unlimited productive and destructive power. We can no longer afford to resolve conflict with violence. This is true not only internationally but for all other forms of disputes.

We need to move to all-win strategies, where all parties end up winning, at every level of society. To achieve this we need new leadership styles. Our personal attitudes, as well as our institutions, are all too often based on psychic or physical violence which is reinforced in all sorts of obvious and subtle ways. We assume that coercion generates more energy than effective cooperation.

The movement away from violence must be accompanied by another vast change in our socioeconomic behavior. For the first time in modern Western history, leaders cannot promise people that their standard of living will rise. Instead, we must shift to a new perspective; we must struggle to increase the quality of life while using fewer resources. Such a goal is quite feasible, but many people must help us find the very different success criteria necessary for this novel task.

The combination of the need for an all-win philosophy and the movement away from maximum economic growth directly threatens the view of most of the current leaders in the Western world. Their vision has inevitably been formed by the values of the industrial era. The problem is enhanced because young people who see the new necessities are blocked from bringing their fresh perspectives to bear by the ever lengthening life spans of those in power.

So where do we go from here? Most people who see that the directions of the world are dangerous tend to blame current leaders, arguing that they have evil motives. This leads to polarization and reinforces the vision that only violence can break through the blocks to a better society. In reality, the primary clash is between those who have perceived the new realities and are proposing that we deal with them and those who have not. New ideas can be communicated only when people are open. We now know that physical or mental threats close minds rather than open them.

For example, the failures of the Reagan administration do not result because the president is evil and wants to cause societal breakdown. There is, on the contrary, ample evidence that he is a good man. The core tragedy is that he and his staff do not understand the fundamental implications of the weaponry revolution, environmental limitations, human rights demands, computer changes, and biological knowledge. Attempts to do good, coupled with wide ignorance of reality, inevitably set up dangerous consequences.

This problem is not confined, of course, to the president or to the United States. Most leaders of countries throughout the world continue to act as though the industrial system can continue. The media, as well as academic and political systems, still primarily reinforce obsolete models and understandings of leadership.   OOO

Teaching New Leadership Styles

A basic problem of the industrial era has been the belief that only one view of reality and one pattern of perception are valid. This viewpoint is less dominant in Europe because of the degree of ethnic and political diversity on that continent compared to the United States.

Many Americans still do not understand that one can see the past, present, and future through profoundly different sets of lenses. The lack of variety of thought in the United States has led to many of the problems which now exist. In fact, the attempt to create a melting pot and eliminate the diversity of immigrants has been a negative factor in the development of the United States.

Diversity is a strength rather than a weakness in a time of rapid and profound shifts. One critical danger in any dynamic process of change is that a primary question will escape the attention of decision-makers and will therefore blindside them. The more types and styles of thought available in thinking through an issue, the more likely it is that nothing crucial will be missed.

We must also realize, however, that diversity without a commitment to cooperation and to a binding core of commonly held basic values can lead to massive cultural strife and breakdown. This pattern has caused the split between the Basques of Northern Spain and the Spanish government. Similar ethnic strife could also develop in the United States as various minorities become more and more powerful.

We need new styles of leadership if we are to cope with the challenges of diversity. Fortunately the number of educational opportunities for leaders is growing throughout the world. All too often, however, we are teaching people current top-down styles and skills of leadership. These are the very patterns which maintain current perceptions and problems.

We need to find opportunities to learn together those new styles of leadership which will be effective in a very diverse world. We can start by searching for all who are willing to lead. We need to break through our traditional prejudices which make it easier for us to see leaders if they are white, middle-aged, middle or upper-class, and male. We need to understand the potential of the young and the old, of women, of minorities, of the poor.

Our blocks on this issue are at two primary levels. First, because we are used to white, male leadership, many find it difficult to see women and minorities as competent. More critically, there are major style differences between female and male as well as between minority and white behavior. Only as we recognize the need for borrowing from all styles, meshing strengths while minimizing weaknesses, can we develop our real potential.

It is difficult enough to involve all groups in decision-making. We need, however, to go further by recognizing how our decision-making styles and the places where we hold meetings reinforce the patterns we so urgently need to change. Informal communication between diverse groups is less likely to occur in corporate board rooms, city council chambers and country clubs.

Power models are so central to our culture that we find it very difficult to consider alternatives. Suggestions for significant change are therefore often dismissed as naive or bizarre. Despite our democratic rhetoric, we do not really believe that people can operate effectively by consensus. The existence of an ongoing Quaker tradition, which operates without power and through persuasion, is dismissed as an interesting curiosity rather than studied as a forerunner of the patterns we can create.

Up to the current time most of our democratic forms imply the tyranny of the majority over the minority. The next step in governance is to recognize that people do not have to be constrained to live within a single set of norms and that coercion can be minimized in a culture of diversity. Moving beyond our current styles will be extraordinarily difficult. The persistence of obsolete social patterns and structures, despite clear evidence of their breakdown, testifies vividly to the strength of current models of reality and decision-making. When we do decide to change, we find that even our buildings tend to constrain us—attesting to the reality of Winston Churchill's aphorism, "We build our buildings and then our buildings build us." Those who have tried to learn *with* people know how the structure of the traditional classroom or church or city hall impedes cooperative and facilitative processes. Similarly, our languages constrain thought and action in ways we are only just beginning to understand.

We need diversity in our leadership if we are to manage a world of diversity. But we must also be fully aware that effective leaders share a commitment which distinguishes them from others who choose not to lead. They are prepared to take risks and know that they will often be wrong. After all, creating the future demands experimentation and nobody is infallible.

The parallels and differences between the leadership styles of today and those of the past are endlessly fascinating. Great leaders have always been able to inspire people and to help change the realities of those who have chosen to commit to their activities. For example, Winston Churchill gathered up the energies of the British people after Dunkirk in World War II and created what is still seen as a miracle of resistance.

The key difference is that most of the styles and structures of society could be expected to remain stable in previous centuries. *Leaders tried to alter events within a basically fixed context. Today, everything is in flux.* The contemporary leader must understand reality well enough to work with others in the rapids of change, while creating long-run support for a fundamentally changed, value-based future.   ○○○

People Are Ready for Change

One primary block to effective action today is the strongly held belief that the general public is not ready to accept fundamentally new thinking. Professionals, bureaucrats, and politicians are particularly likely to advance this view. My experience shows that, on the contrary, there is general recognition that past ideas and models are obsolete.

As one might expect, most individuals would love to discover a neat set of answers to their individual and societal problems. But when change agents state upfront that nobody has tidy responses to our complex questions, people are willing to sit down and talk about the dangers and the potentials we face. The difficulty, however, is that the closer we get to the systems that currently control the movement of information—the media and educational organizations—the less likely we are to encounter people who value work in a questioning mode rather than in terms of answers.

I am often confronted with blank disbelief when I make positive statements about public attitudes. Many people are simply unwilling to believe that I can raise tough issues with the general public and that they will respond not only with interest but enthusiasm. When I tell public policy analysts that I discuss fundamental change issues with rural audiences in the heartland of America, they are inclined to call me a liar!

For example, I was able to introduce fundamentally new ideas when visiting northern Wisconsin, a depressed area of the state. We examined the way in which people who had fallen behind in paying their property taxes could work for the county to pay off their debts. Since then, the concept has been developed into a possible work program. Debtors could cut wood in the state and national forests, which produce more timber than is being used. This wood would then be given to those entitled to fuel aid from the federal government. The money which would have gone outside the state would be made available to the counties to pay off past due taxes so that property will not be lost. While there is no guarantee that this model will be implemented, it is clear that the people involved *are* ready to rethink old positions. A broader barter model is also being successfully used in communities in Canada based on work by *Landsman Associates*; this enables people to exchange goods and services using locally created computer-based currencies in parallel with national money.

Before I started my rural visits, I was deeply concerned about how people would react to my perceptions. But I have now met with enough people and groups to be sure that rural conservatives are open to rethinking directions to achieve their values. People are sick and tired of blind optimism which denies their day-to-day situation. They will listen to those who are realistically hopeful.

This does not mean, however, that people will stomach a diet of gloom. *In a conflict between optimism and pessimism, optimism will win every time.* When the choice is between incredible optimism and hopeful realism, however, many people are ready to think and act. We have grossly underestimated the willingness of people to respond to challenges.

Why are so many of those who claim to be interested in change also committed to the idea that the public is unaware and apathetic? In my more cynical moments, I fear that most "idea" people would be deeply unhappy if they were called upon to actually act. They are content to dream of what should be done. They certainly do not want an opportunity to achieve it.

Reality has an unpleasant way of being more complex and messy than theory. There are no absolutely good or bad moves in the real world. So those who have been seduced by the glorious clarity of ideas all too often find themselves ineffective in the real world. On the other hand, many who see themselves as movers and shakers are not well informed. They operate, in the words of John Maynard Keynes, the great British economist, "as slaves of some dead economist."

There are five basic requirements for effective processes to bring about change:

• We must work with the total leadership regardless of age, sex, creed, color, or class. We need to be aware of the biases which cause us to see certain types of leadership as more effective or more important than others.

• We must ensure that people become aware of the driving forces which make it impossible for activities to be carried out in the same way as in the past. In the absence of information about fundamental change, most people will try to maintain past patterns.

• We must recognize how insider/outsider relationships function. The task of an outsider is often to disrupt the conventional thinking of a group; the task of the insider is to integrate new ideas so that systems can continue to operate.

• We must set up knowledge systems so that it is easier to find information when it is needed. We must move beyond current patterns which monopolize knowledge, and ensure it is broadly shared instead.

• We must break down the current separation between study and action. In today's world, these are two faces of a single coin.

We know a great deal about the processes which can help people achieve change. But the first step still lies with the individual. Is he or she prepared to open up to new inputs, insights and understandings? And how can we provide the environments in which this can be done most effectively?

I am often asked whether a particular change is possible. I respond by saying that this is the wrong question. Instead, each of us needs to ask where our commitment is and where we shall act. Once we are committed, we will find ways to be effective.   OOO

Creating New Knowledge Structures

One central reality of today's world is information over-load, also called by the colorful term infoglut.

How can we reduce infoglut? One step would be to stop encouraging people to publish when they have nothing to say. Professors are often promoted on the basis of how *much* they write rather than how *relevantly* they work. If they do not publish, professors are often denied tenure or promotion. Therefore, few feel they can afford to take on complex and worthwhile research when there is no guarantee that it will result in publishable material.

We are still operating on the basis that more information services, more books, and more TV channels are good in themselves. In other words, we are still assuming that the problem is providing access to the scarce resource of information. We shall only really learn to cope with infoglut when we recognize that the key need is to help people find the *specific* information they want at the moment they want it.

Assailed by complex, contradictory and excessive infor-mation, many people have given up any hope of under-standing the world in which they live. Citizens assume they cannot hope to make sense of complex issues because even "experts" are unable to agree on desirable directions.

Decision-makers are caught in the same bind. They find themselves unable to move, as special interests clash without caring about the larger picture. Few individuals, and fewer groups, are devoted to seeking the general good even in theory, let alone in practice. And those who do look for broader benefits have little credibility in the society and even less with policy makers.

Fortunately, some decision-makers and leaders are increasingly aware of our policy-making paralysis. Even more critically, they are coming to realize that their own conclusions are based on their personal and partial understanding of reality. These social entrepreneurs are struggling to find new ways to test their understandings. They want to be sure that the proposals they make will be helpful rather than destructive.

This hunger for dialogue rather than confrontation was dramatically confirmed at a meeting I attended with top members of several religious denominations in Iowa late in 1985. There was profound concern about the human pain and suffering in the state. However, many of those who had previously been most active in struggling for one specific form of action to benefit the deprived had realized that conditions were still getting worse despite their best efforts.

They had started to look for better information which would provide a sense of the leverage points so they could be more effective. System theorists now know that there are only a few places where complex systems are vulnerable to change. A growing group is struggling to determine when effort is being wasted and when it will have effects out of proportion to the energy employed.

Taking agriculture as an example, we can list just a few of the many questions which need serious study before we determine what policies will and will not make a difference. Will it be possible to increase American food and fiber exports again, or will countries tend to become more self-sufficient? Will other rich countries continue to develop surpluses which they will sell abroad? Will the developing countries continue to lose ground agriculturally? Would higher food and fiber prices benefit or cost the American farmer over the long-run? Is the long-term fertility of the land being damaged by current cropping patterns? Should heavy use of fertilizer and pesticides be discouraged at the risk of reducing yields? Are large corporate farms more or less cost effective than the family farm? And at the overall level: will the climate change dramatically?

Current systems of research and debate tend to continue, and even worsen, the differences of opinion around these questions. We need to create new knowledge structures which would help us discover what the evidence shows and what needs to be done to clarify disagreements, and then devise alternative scenarios which people of good will can discuss. A number of structures are being developed to ensure this pattern—the one I know best is called *the problem/possibility focuser*. In this process, a group of people who are more interested in discovering the truth than in preserving their current understandings get together and decide:

1. What are the current agreements among those who have studied a particular issue realistically rather than ideologically?

2. What are the disagreements and why do they exist? Do people operate on different "factual" bases, hold different views about likely trends, or see the nature of the environment from divergent stances? Have they different understandings of the nature of humanity, or do they have varied ultimate beliefs about the universe?

3. What is the most probable scenario for the future? What would change this scenario? How would it feel to live within the proposed scenario?

4. What study resources are available for those who would like to learn more?

The resulting document is an educational tool, one which teaches people how to think. It should be kept up-to-date and be made available for discussion, not only in print but also in audio and video forms. Games and simulations should also be used to make it easier for people to grasp the major points of importance. Each document should be produced for various levels of comprehension. In fact, I believe that the next type of encyclopedia will be based on clarifying questions and contexts, as is done in the problem/possibility focuser, rather than on providing answers.

Developing a problem/possibility focuser takes significant time and commitment. Once a clearer picture has been defined, however, many effective tools are available to show which policy directions will have favorable impacts and which will be ineffective in moving toward defined goals.

Once people understand realistic choices, they can decide in what direction they would like to move. The problem/possibility focuser fits well within a servant leadership world. It enables the leader to discover what will be best for the society by bringing together those with competence and knowledge. It assumes that problems can be turned into possibilities when people of good will work together. And finally, it recognizes that we need to change our success criteria.   OOO

Linking Systems

More and more people talk about the need for networking and linkages. It sometimes seems that people believe these styles are essentially new; at other times it seems that the concepts are old, but being used in new ways.

Any useful understanding of networks and linkages must be placed within the context of changing authority structures. Linkages and networks are the way that informal systems have always operated. They are also the channels used when formal authority structures break down. This explains why some bureaucracies, which seem totally fouled up, still manage to get part of their necessary work done. Linkages and networks are also the way that activities get coordinated between systems when the formal communication channels between them are blocked or nonexistent. Traditional "old boy" networks enable effective processes to go on within and between inefficient formal authority structures.

There is nothing new about these types of linkages and networks. Someone probably "knew someone who knew someone" back in Babylonian times! What's new about our situation is that linkages and networks are going to be the primary, and recognized, way to get things done in the future. Structural authority systems based on "power over" will be less and less common.

We are currently making a very bumpy transition from being controlled by top-down power structures to working through linkages and networks. Even those who are most aware of the implications of this shift, and would like to pursue it wholeheartedly, are often ineffective. One block is that there is today no acceptable legal definition of a networking system, where authority has no single locus. Fortunately, people are beginning to struggle with this issue.

The need to use "profit" or "nonprofit" structures is damaging because it disguises the reality that effective linkages and networks cannot be controlled by a single head or group. They depend on everybody taking responsibility and being willing to live up to their commitments. Desired behavior cannot be forced. Disagreements and misunderstandings must be resolved by dialogue and conciliation. Linking and networking systems require a high level of maturity.

Action Linkage, a networking system I have facilitated for nearly twenty years under different names, has shown the strengths and demonstrated the weaknesses of networking. It assumes that all those involved will behave well whether they base their sense of responsibility on the golden rule, or spiritual values, or humanistic beliefs. Our organization, therefore, only functions well when its members behave responsibly.

We have proved that it is possible, even in mass mailings, to offer people the choice of paying less money for services if they cannot afford the full price. Conventional theory would assume that everybody would take advantage of such an offer. But most people will pay the full price if they can afford to do so.

We have, of course, also found that this type of organization is no panacea. We ask people to sign an agreement which states the assumptions on which we work together. But problems emerge when a few people do not meet monetary commitments or, more seriously, fail to complete work to which they have committed. Our greatest disappointment comes when people do not even honor their agreement to find a replacement if they become overloaded or overcommitted as can happen to all of us.

None of these limitations should be advanced as proof that we should abandon our attempt and the many others like it. We live in an imperfect world and we work with imperfect people; this reality will never change. The real question is: "What system maximizes human strengths and minimizes weaknesses?" Shall we get more done by controlling people and preventing them from goofing off using "sticks and carrots?" Or will we be more effective when we challenge people to act on the belief that most healthy people want to grow and help others to grow?

We cannot, however, remain stuck between the old and the new styles of organization for an indefinite time. Does authority emerge from position? Or is it based on competence in particular areas? Our choices will be very different depending on our beliefs.

Authority based on competence is sometimes rejected by those who fear that power would no longer be available to force cohesion in emergencies. In fact, the chain of command will be tighter at such times because people will have given their commitment to an organization or a direction and will be more willing to do what they are told when there is no time for discussion.

After an emergency is over, however, there will be significant differences in how the situation is evaluated. In a structural authority system, the strong tendency is to enforce the authority of the person who was in charge, *regardless of whether the decision was right or wrong.*

In a sapiential authority system, the search is to discover what really happened so that the error can be corrected and the chance for a similar error reduced. If this requires that there must be a change in leaders, this will be accepted and even welcomed. The commitment is to the *truth* rather than to the structure. The reaction to the blowup of the space shuttle Challenger, and other similar crises, suggests that we are moving out of the structural authority world which has controlled us during the industrial era, and toward a search for the truth. The confessions and confusions that emerge as society moves in this direction are vital, even though they are often painful.   OOO

The Scales
of Change

How many times do we state, or imply, that there is only one type of activity that will bring about change? We press for individual learning or community development or global peace, and we ignore the reality that all these levels are interconnected and must be affected at once.

It makes sense for most of us to concentrate on one issue and one scale of action. But we ourselves become blocks to effective change when we deny that the priorities of others are as important as our own. We prevent synergy when we look at a narrow spectrum of reality rather than broadening our perspectives.

The material in this section deals with the scales at which change operates, and the different models which are available. However, the block to action today is not a lack of action possibilities. Rather it is our lack of personal and social commitment. The right question is, "Are we willing to act?" rather than, "Is it possible?"

Individual Balance

The ultimate problem in personal autonomy was posed by St. Paul in his tragic statement: "The things I would not do, those I do. The things I would do, those I do not." This is the heart of the human dilemma. When I try to live the examined life, I am inevitably dismayed by the capacity of my mind/body to frustrate my best intentions. I resolve to give up a bad habit and nothing I do seems to overcome past patterns. Fortunately we are learning new ways to align with ourselves or, to use the colloquial, to "get our act together."

Nobody can work or live well with others when they do not accept their own weaknesses or are booby trapped by their own contradictions. Those who quote the text, "Thou shalt love thy neighbor as thyself" usually place the emphasis in the wrong place. You cannot love and accept your neighbor until you love and accept yourself. Until you learn to *love yourself*, you filter all incoming communication through your own narrow perceptions and needs. Most people use a very narrow set of filters through which they see and listen. They do not perceive the richness of the "other" or what they can learn from those who have different parts of the picture.

Loving yourself does *not* mean that you *like* everything about yourself. The most effective way to get rid of bad habits is not by fighting them, but by finding something more important which grows into the space previously occupied by what you dislike. Self love, in this deep sense, provides the courage to make moves in desirable directions. Then you can slough off the undesirable. Elimination of the negative without cultivation of the positive simply creates a vacuum into which other destructive patterns will often grow.

The search for maturity is, of course, never ending. It is like the climb you make to the top of a "mountain" only to find that it was a foothill. But the climb itself becomes the reward, and the knowledge that it can never be completed, the ultimate tension. What do you learn as you climb? You learn to live in dynamic balance. You gain a better knowledge of reality, which limits mistakes and ensures that you are less often blindsided by the unexpected. You also learn to avoid outside control of your life and excessive use of external stimuli, such as chemicals.

As you become healthier, you discover an innate desire to grow and help others to grow. This does not mean that people stop making mistakes and hurting themselves and others. It does not mean that people will always move in the best directions. It does mean that we shall get more done when we work with other individuals and groups rather than against them. We need to challenge people to find their potential rather than force them to behave the way we want through our sticks and carrots.

As people become healthier, they discover how they are trapped by their own perceptions and their limitations. We can find alternative universes with better choices if we break out of our current limited visions. Discovering how to move beyond the barriers we set for ourselves is one primary challenge of our times. As we meet it, we will be less likely to be forced to do what we do not want to do.

Growth and development are positive. But they are also stressful. Giving up anything is always costly. This is particularly true when you have to abandon cherished old beliefs which you have used to make sense of the world. Few of us can achieve real forward movement without one or more "dark nights of the soul." This rhetoric may be too highly colored for some to cope with easily. But personal growth is primarily an emotional and not an analytic process and none of us escapes despair, anger, and grief along the way. It is at this point that we need to join with others in support groups, so we can turn our personal crises into effective change.

As we grow, we see the potential for personal leadership, for becoming a small scale hero or heroine. The ideal of being a hero or heroine in our own life is new for many of us. All too often we confuse this role with that of the martyr who is willing to suffer or die for the cause. I strongly believe, however, that we should run a mile away from a willing martyr. While people sometimes must suffer or die for their cause, it should not normally be seen as positive, because our greatest need today is to find out how we can use conflict to promote creativity rather than violence.

This moves us beyond the work of Gandhi and Martin Luther King. They learned how to turn violence back on those who offered it and to shame them into altering their behavior. Today we must learn how to defuse the misunderstandings, and anger, which are the inevitable result of our move from the industrial era to the compassionate era. We must learn that inciting others to violence is as "violent" as acting aggressively ourselves.

This need for new definitions of nonviolence is one of the frontiers of our time. Its implications have not yet been recognized so our models for individual and social change still primarily emerge from confrontation. We need to search for styles which invite people to be involved rather than making them feel like outsiders and inferior. However much any of us have grown, we are all on the journey throughout our lives. We need to commit ourselves to strengthening all those we come in contact with, rather than pointing out and even rejoicing over their weaknesses. Groups such as *The Focusing Institute* and *Search for Common Ground* are struggling with these issues.

This need to support people rather than weaken them parallels what we are learning in cancer research. Up to now, many therapies which tried to kill cancer cells weakened the body's own defenses as a side effect. But today doctors are searching for ways to strengthen the body so that it will fight for itself, thus supporting health rather than fighting illness. Similarly, we need to reinforce health in ourselves and others as individuals. This is the new and highly exciting perspective of the eighties.   OOO

The Family

Our family patterns are very different from those of the past. Human beings tended to rear their families in very similar ways throughout the world until the industrial revolution. Young people were typically surrounded by large extended families. In addition to mothers and fathers and siblings, other relatives almost always lived nearby. Many people were responsible for the young and for the old. If one person died or got sick or failed to deal with responsibilities for other reasons, the slack would be picked up elsewhere.

The primary changes in family patterns in our Western culture have resulted from technological shifts. First, the development of increasingly rapid transportation made it possible for people to move away from their relatives rather than being rooted in their communities. In the nineteenth century, people travelled long distances, but then typically put down roots again and stayed where they arrived. In the twentieth century, people change their homes far more often. In fact, high levels of mobility are a critical part of current American life. In Europe, mobility is still far more limited, and distances are usually shorter so extended families can get together from time to time.

The increase in mobility created a new grouping known as the "nuclear family." The idealized version in the mid-twentieth century was a father, mother, and two children. Those who were not married, or did not have children, had a hard time fitting into the society.

This vision persists although fewer and fewer families are structured in this way. People get married later in their lives. Many married couples decide not to have children. Even if there are young children, both husband and wife often hold jobs. Finally, more and more people live together without being married.

The dramatic decreases in the numbers of births per 1000 women in the rich countries have been partly due to changes in lifestyle, partly due to the increasing cost of raising children, partly due to the perceived danger of overpopulation, and partly due to safe and effective contraception. The increase in sexual freedom and other factors has led to an enormous rise in the divorce rate. Now, more and more families are headed by single parents, most of them women, and many are in poverty.

Society is now adjusting to current trends, despite the fact that nobody planned for them and many people have severe doubts about the long-run viability of our emerging system. This willingness to adjust may not be the wisest course, however, because there are already signs of reversals to earlier patterns. Many people are deciding that we need more supportive family styles if we are to maximize the quality of life in the future.

What changes in directions are already visible? For one, the freewheeling sexual habits of the seventies are under challenge from those who want to re-create more traditional families. In addition, health threats from AIDS and other sexually transmitted diseases are curtailing sexual license. Even those who led the sexual revolution are now arguing that they were wrong to stress only the sexual act.

The definition of family has also been shifting again. In today's world, extended families are not necessarily related by blood. A whole new category of "fictive" kin has developed. People care deeply about "grandparents" and "parents" and "children," even though they may know each other only because they live in the same community.

Other shifts in patterns can be confidently anticipated. The greatest alteration will occur as we accept fully that women can bear more children than the world can support; the only question is regarding the patterns which will be developed to cut back on births. China has already decided that families should not have more than one child. Singapore has related the right to have children to the IQ of the parents.

What will we do in the rich countries? I hope we shall encourage people to have children only if they are committed to rearing them so they reach their full potential. People would then be challenged by society to think deeply about the requirements of effective child rearing before they make the decision to have babies. I am not arguing for government control or licensing, which I would consider disastrous. I am suggesting that our educational patterns need to encourage people to think about all the implications of having children before making the choice to do so.

The labor saving impact of computers and robots will enable us to move toward a society in which those who have children can be free to concentrate on this responsibility for a period of years. We must recognize that child rearing is a major task, requiring commitment from both fathers and mothers.

If people see their career as more important than children, they will do well to let others be parents and choose to serve as fictive aunts and uncles. Those who raise children can also choose demanding work outside the family at other points in their lives. With our advancing technology, there will be time in tomorrow's world for child rearing, social entrepreneurship, work and joy.   OOO

The Entrepreneurial Neighborhood and Community

The current interest in entrepreneurial communities can be traced back to many sources, but notably to three types of futures programs. The goals programs started in Los Angeles, but the most visible example was "Goals for Dallas" which took place in the early seventies. This program made proposals—developed by a very rich and very powerful citizen—for building the city. People in the area were given a chance to make comments on the program but few changes were made as a result of the feedback. The process did, however, begin to teach people how to talk about choices.

Many communities followed Dallas's lead. They typically achieved less because their leaders had less clout in the communities. In addition, as citizens became more sophisticated, they began to ask why their input had so little influence on directions.

Later goals efforts overlapped with a second type of approach found in Iowa 2000, Hawaii 2000, Seattle 2000, Alternatives for Washington, and many others. I was involved in many of these efforts and saw some of their strengths and their weaknesses at first hand. They did succeed in educating a number of key leaders about the changing realities of our time, and in introducing new thinking into the communities and states.

One weakness was that these efforts recruited, almost exclusively, the people who have traditionally been defined as leaders, with emphasis on middle-aged, well-off males. A more serious limitation was that the projects typically ended with reports being made to a legislature or city council and being filed there. These elected groups were often not interested in what had been done nor aware of its potential importance.

The third type of program was designed to teach leadership skills within communities and states. Initial leadership programs tended to reinforce existing patterns of thinking and behavior because they were largely taught by traditional leaders and failed to discuss the discontinuities in our culture. Recently, however, leadership programs are changing their nature and meshing with the idea of the entrepreneurial community. This concept is developing in a number of areas, particularly in the heartland of the country.

The effective creation of an entrepreneurial community demands that three rules be observed. The first is to ensure that all the leadership of a community is involved, whether participants fit traditional definitions of leaders or not. The second is to make sure that everybody becomes fully aware of the driving forces which cause change, so that individuals learn why it is impossible to continue in conventional directions. The third is to ensure that those who develop ideas are also responsible for their implementation.

Many believe that decisions should be made as closely as possible to the where people are who are affected by them. There is more and more agreement that the drift of power from local governments to state and national centers has been ill advised. A reversal of this trend demands, however, that communities be willing to make the tough decisions which are required to ensure equity and justice.

The unwillingness of communities to face ethical dilemmas was the primary reason why power moved to the state and national level. We dare not reverse this pattern before communities are ready to be concerned about all citizens, male and female, young and old, and those of all races. It is only when local communities commit to servant leadership that we shall be able to bring decision-making authority back to them. We shall then manage diversity by working within communities rather than imposing central programs on them.

There is, of course, still strong resistance to moving back to community-based decision-making. Many planners and policymakers continue to believe that there is *only one best way* to solve problems. They therefore force identical solutions on everybody.

The bigger block to the needed shift, however, is our unwillingness to tolerate failure. If we use local decision-making, some neighborhoods and communities will inevitably make mistakes and a few may fail catastrophically. This cost must be accepted. It is better for some communities and neighborhoods to take the wrong direction rather than risk the *total* culture going over the waterfall.

We cannot be sure what we should be doing as individuals, families, and communities. The lack of clear-cut criteria for effective action in today's conditions makes people profoundly nervous about their choices. Still, we can help overcome this difficulty by encouraging experimentation and spreading information about successful models.

Encouraging community autonomy implies profound changes in style. Communities today have many patterns imposed on them from outside. If they were encouraged to discover their real felt needs, they would challenge many patterns which are now taken for granted. For example, doubt would be cast on the interpretation of a number of constitutional clauses such as the commerce clause which prohibits interruption of trade. We would re-examine our thinking, asking, for example, if a community or state is entitled to block economic growth if this would enhance the community's quality of life.

Most discussions in recent years have assumed that the interests of the nation-state are more important that those of communities, states, and bioregions. This view is challenged by our new understandings. But the traumas involved in moving power away from the national level will go very deep.   OOO

The Bioregion

The lines that surveyors drew to allow efficient administration are slowly giving way to ecological realities. The process is slow and difficult but it is also irresistible. The boundaries between counties, states and nations are less and less
critical as environmental pressures force new decision-
making patterns.

One can see these shifts producing severe tensions at the
state level. For example, Oregon and Washington each have
two profoundly different ecological realities: both have wet
coasts and dry inland plateaus. The policies developed by
and for the most powerful part of the state are often counterproductive for the rest. There is, as yet, no effective way to
manage these differences. In a similar way, the needs of the
Highlands of Scotland and those of southern England are
profoundly different. Indeed, the needs of the highland, the
islands, and the lowlands of Scotland all diverge from each
other.

Regional realities are forcing cooperation between states
and nations. For example, jurisdiction over the Great Lakes
is, of course, divided between the United States and Canada.
But the current very high water levels and the attempt of
the Southwestern states to buy water are forcing ever-closer
collaboration between the two countries.

National statistics fail to illuminate the complex realities
of various regions. The crosscurrents running in America
and all the nations of the world are so fierce that looking at
totals and averages is extremely misleading. The rural areas
of the agricultural and oil states in North America are today
in a recession, even a slump. Most urban centers, including
even those in the depressed states, are still doing reasonably
well, although Dallas and Houston have had to limit their
high flying ways dramatically due to the oil price collapse.

The tensions within states and regions are not based just
on ecological and bioregional issues. Patterns of thinking are

also strongly influenced by the centers to which people relate. The city of Denver in Colorado, not Omaha or Lincoln in Nebraska itself, holds the interests and loyalties of western Nebraskans. We need to be conscious of similarly growing problems caused by the clashes between geographical lines drawn on maps and the bioregional and ecological realities emerging not only in America but throughout the world.

Tensions are becoming more and more severe. One example is the shopping patterns in many areas. Increasingly, both shopping and services are centralized, draining ever more resources from the rural areas. Because small town stores offer limited merchandise, residents shop in the larger town. Stores go bankrupt; the small town loses more of its population base because demand is now insufficient to support even minimal services. In turn, larger towns are threatened by cities because consumers can find a larger selection of goods and also be entertained. Finally, cities, especially downtowns, are threatened by huge regional malls, which pull people from hundreds of miles away. The current drop in gas prices will reinforce these trends, although an eventual reversal is inevitable.

Industrial-era styles of decision-making and governance relied on clear boundaries and the power to make unambiguous decisions. Today communities, states, and nations are being forced to give up sovereignty to work together on some of the most critical issues of our time. For example, water policy necessarily requires regional compacts; moreover, the dangers of acid rain must be examined on a worldwide scale, as shown by the recent United States-Canada and Britain-Scandinavia pacts.

At the other end of the scale, community autonomy will be appropriate only if it is balanced by an increased understanding of regional interdependence. One of the threats of the future is excessive isolation between communities. A good deal of our future decision-making time will be taken up helping people and groups discover the scale on which directions can be effectively decided.

The borders of ad hoc bioregional decision-making groups will seldom be identical for varying purposes. This will make authority lines even less clear. Power tactics are ineffective in unclear and "slippery" management systems. Instead, competence and knowledge must be used to manage the overlaps in decision-making authority and structures.

How do the concerns discussed above mesh with the ongoing attempt to consolidate the excessive number of governmental bodies so that lines of authority can be clarified? The drive to consolidate has been in place for years, indeed decades, and has met with very strong resistance. I believe that the only hope for significant progress is to develop a new set of organizational principles to replace current models. As we take this step, we shall introduce new styles and scales of government which will be clearly superior and cheaper. They will then attract the loyalty of both citizens and those who govern. We will not consolidate; rather we shall reorganize to promote *leadership* rather than management.

We still usually think of governance in terms of a group of people who make policies for others. The new forms of decision-making suggested here will encourage people and institutions to react effectively to emerging realities. People can make good decisions for themselves, individually and in groups, if they know what their choices really are.

Effective bioregional activities do not cut across natural systems but work with them, intervening at points where maximum impact can be achieved with minimum input of effort and resources. Those of us who want to support positive dynamics and destroy negative ones must become far more skillful. We need to understand styles and techniques which support change both within human systems and ecologically.   OOO

The Global Overview

We have always defined reality in win-lose terms. This attitude started with intertribal fighting. Then cities had conflicts with other cities. When we moved to the nation-state level, we divided ourselves with one country proclaiming the wickedness of all others. The United States states that the Soviet State is "an evil empire" and the Soviets reciprocate in kind.

In the 1960s, I believed that I'd come up with an answer to this win-lose system! We could create a "Martian threat." Everybody would unite to fight the mythical Martians and we would get beyond the struggles of the nation-states. Interestingly, there were reports that President Reagan made the same suggestion to General Secretary Mikhail Gorbachev during their 1985 face-to-face meeting in Geneva.

There is, unfortunately, a critical flaw in this idea. So long as we maintain the perception that one side to a conflict must lose and the other side must win, there will still be violence on earth. Given that the nations of the world would have become "officially" united against the Martians, we would have had to search for the causes of discord elsewhere. Inevitably, we would decide that it was Martian spies who were causing the difficulties and we would persecute people we believed had sold out to the space aliens.

We must break through our win-lose perceptions of reality. One block to making necessary changes is our belief that international violence through terrorism and war has a quite different quality and pattern than internal violence. We need to face the fact that violence is an intrinsic part of our industrial-era cultures, both internally and externally.

Even our governmental structures are violent in nature. We live within systems where majorities can impose their will on minorities. We still believe that it is appropriate for a dominant group of people to force their beliefs on others.

Almost all of the current thinking about the long-run direction of our global society argues that a world government would have essentially the same style and pattern as current national governments.

World-order discussions usually assume that we shall shift coercive power from the national level to the global level. On the contrary, the real need is to move beyond the idea that coercion is the best way to get things done. We must discover how people and nations can work with fundamental diversity, seeking creative solutions to conflict and reserving coercive power for exceptional situations.

Once we understand this profoundly new direction, we discover that we are further along in building a global system than we normally recognize. We are already effectively networking people who share the vision of an all-win society. These people are learning to work together in an intricately linked system which will be managed through common ground and open space discussions. This whole system is beginning to be visible through a complex relationship of committed people and non-governmental institutions operating on a transnational scale. We are being drawn together by the necessities of a shrinking planet.

Transportation has obviously brought the world closer. But we are only now grasping that distance has, for many purposes, been totally eliminated by the communications revolution. Cities on different continents are today as "close" as places within a country or state. The global village already exists. Most older people still have difficulty perceiving its reality, but many young people recognize it instinctively.

The nation-state is therefore no longer an effective decision-making body. No single country can operate outside international realities even today. The need for coherent decision-making is now spreading from economics to environmental and ecological issues.

One of the first fruits of the space age was the picture of the earth as a serene, beautiful, blue globe. These photographs were one of the triggers helping people see that we needed to live in peace. We often ask ourselves whether we shall move toward a shared world vision, but this is the wrong question. *Instead, we need to ask whether we will commit to thought and action in time to avoid catastrophe.*

People resist the idea of global discussions because they assume that it will decrease their control of their own lives. This perception is unrealistic. Effective worldwide governance will only be feasible if we keep most decision-making on the local level. When issues are genuinely wider than the local area, they should move up the scale to bioregions, then continents. Decisions should only be taken to the global level when *absolutely* necessary.

Existing nation-states will be emotional anchors for people for many decades into the future. But people will also take on other critical commitments. They will work with their communities to create a high quality of life. They will care about the ecological stability of their bioregion. They will search for ways to meet human needs throughout the world.

Movement to higher levels of organization and skills is part of our upward evolutionary spiral. In one sense, the movement beyond the nation-state to a global level is part of a long-run trend. Seen from a different perspective, this shift marks the end of human adolescence and the development of maturity. The nation-state was a functional unit in the industrial era. It will not be effective in a world which can be destroyed by the careless use of our unlimited productive and destructive power. Only a commitment to effective dialogue, diversity, and spiritual values can ensure our survival in these new conditions.   OOO

SECTION 5

The Skills of Change

All of us carry around unconscious assumptions about appropriate forms of behavior. Many of them prevent us from bringing about the changes we claim we want to achieve.

The shorter sections which follow take brief statements that my wife or I have developed, or borrowed from others. They then provide catchy, teachable concepts. More and more people believe that aphorisms are the quickest way to convey new truths. This is the approach used here.

Some may see these ideas as too simple. I believe that at the end of every intellectual journey lies common sense. Simple ideas are best if they convey truth.

The findings of many of these statements reflect my personal journey. The word "I" is therefore used far more extensively here than in other parts of the book.

People Always Act in
Their Perceived Self-Interest

The startling implications of the title to this piece are not yet widely understood. All too many people confuse self-interest with selfishness. The person who mugs someone to get money for drugs is acting in his or her perceived self-interest, but so is the man or woman who saves a child at the risk of his or her own life. Individuals have different visions of appropriate behavior given their upbringing, needs and values; this will cause them to choose either creative or destructive directions.

An expansion of this statement describes the ways in which communities can be influenced. All of us who have worked in community development have realized that we must start with the felt self-interest needs of those in the community. If we start by helping people achieve something they see as worthwhile, they may then decide that we are trustworthy and start listening to other possibilities we believe are important.

Social change requires that we either appeal to the existing self-interest of individuals and groups, or help them gain different perceptions of their self-interest. This, in turn, requires change agents to have three skills. First, they must know how to learn what an individual, group or community currently believes is important, credible and relevant. A proposal which cuts across current self-images will not be adopted. For example, I once made a suggestion that Nebraska should struggle to redefine the meaning of work. This was seen as reducing the commitment to the work ethic; I was firmly informed that such an idea would not fly.

The second requirement is to identify what directions an individual or group might find exciting. Directions which some people find relevant and positive may be seen by others as damaging. There must be a positive vision if energy is to be mobilized. But the vision must be refined and redefined over time if it is to continue to mesh with the realities created by rapid change.

Finally, change agents must communicate new ideas to people in language they can understand. How many of you have been frustrated listening to a person who uses jargon, ideas which you find unacceptable, or jokes which you see as ugly? How many of you have listened in awe as a speaker or presenter has managed to make the best of a seemingly "impossible" case—making bricks without straw? Presentations may place an individual firmly in the enemy camp, or they may help people see new realities of benefit to them.

These three skills will enable individuals and groups to discover what their current self-interests are, define where they need to be changed, and recognize how to make the necessary shifts. When people change their perception of their self-interests, their behavior inevitably changes.   OOO

Perceptions and Thoughts Determine Actions

Dialogue and discussion are often dismissed as "just talk" and a waste of time. This reaction is most common from go-getter action types. Americans often react this way because they want to "get on with it" rather than spend time thinking through the potentials and dangers .

This is the natural approach of a culture based on power which assumes that only position and influence alter reality. Thought and action can, however, be changed through interaction between people who see the world differently.

The Japanese have recognized the importance of talk and dialogue in their management systems. New ideas and directions are discussed at length before being introduced. The extra time given to the preparatory process is usually more than offset by the fact that people act effectively once a decision is made. The British civil service uses a variant of this technique. The most junior person is required to react to a situation first. This judgment is refined as those with more experience make their views known. The old get the advantage of freshness of view and the young learn why their initial answer may not work based on experience.

Talk and action need to balance each other, of course. Cultures and groups which tend to talk need to be encouraged to act, and those which tend to act before thinking need to be urged to reflect. In the days when I did a great deal of campus visiting, I discovered fascinating differences between various types of colleges. At Catholic campuses, it was relatively easy to create high level intellectual discussion, but very hard to get follow-though. Most other campuses wanted to move to action immediately, but commitment was seldom sustained because there was no conceptual base.

Thought is a necessary prelude to action today. Most fundamental change activities break down because those involved in them do not take the time to gain a shared model of reality. The members of the group are pulled apart by tensions caused by the rapids of change. Only a coherent, shared vision can support a group through the inevitable compromises which are required as we move a vision into reality.

Thought does influence and cause action. I have occasionally run a seminar where people have suddenly perceived a fundamentally new reality. One of the most dramatic examples was with the Young Presidents' Organization when those attending learned the reality of ecological limits and changed their fundamental view of success and their personal values. When I met with them a year later, they complained that they no longer sought the company of many whom they had previously enjoyed.

Once we fully understand that our perceptions only convey part of the total reality, we shall be ready to work with others who seem to differ from us.   OOO

Healthy Relationships Depend on Individual Maturity

Maturity in one's perception of personal self-interest is essential for good relationships with other people. You can only provide other people with enough space for their own journey if you do not need to confirm your own ego needs.

Ayn Rand is one author who has challenged people to take an autonomous stand to recognize their own potential. Regrettably, she has largely destroyed the positive value of her work by failing to recognize that empowered individuals should seek to work with other competent people rather than maintain power over them.

We have now learned that nothing important can be achieved today without working *with* others. The stronger an individual, the less necessary it is for him or her to show power, because it will be visible in both thought and action patterns.

Healthy relationships show a pattern which moves far beyond our industrial-era thinking and understandings. I used to ask myself whether an action I was taking in a friendship or my marriage was selfish or selfless. I came to understand, over time, that these terms are meaningless if the friendship or relationship is truly grounded. I am no longer looking at the effect on one individual or another but at the impact on the total system.

There is, however, no shortcut to mature relationships. Each of us must grow to the point where we can give up the need for short-run and immediate gratification. We must recognize that giving and taking need to be balanced.

This is *not* a plea for unselfishness with the consequent feeling of moral superiority. Nor am I suggesting we adopt the ridiculous patterns which emerge when people are not willing to say what they want because they don't want to impose their will. What is needed is a willingness to work long and hard to learn what will benefit both, or all, the parties in a relationship.

Just as individual success in discovering who one is can produce those rare moments of feeling in tune with the universe, successful developments in relationships bring a sense of quiet, and sometimes boisterous, happiness.

Many mystics have written about those moments when they can see every human being and all of nature as connected. Even those who are more hardheaded can appreciate, in theoretical terms, the extraordinary web of relationships which keep us alive.

As always, we need a sense of balance. Each of us is a tiny part of the universe, but what we do certainly affects those immediately around us and often many more people. We need to live and act in ways which honor our capacities and the needs of those around us.   OOO

Everything You Do is Critical, but You Could be Wrong

Leadership is under attack in our culture. We no longer admire great men and women, but look for their flaws.

We need leaders, however, to help us see the need for new directions and thus make our way through the rapids of change. A necessary and profound shift is, therefore, taking place in leadership models. Today's leaders, whether individually or in groups, need to be open to the possibility that they may be wrong. Leaders need to be committed to bringing about change, but they also must be aware that their vision will inevitably be inadequate, incomplete, and, at times, incorrect.

This requires an extraordinary balancing act. Leaders must be aware that everything they do is *critically important*. They draw their commitment and drive from this understanding, and also support others through their enthusiasm and courage. But they must also be aware that they *may be wrong*, for this will encourage them to welcome feedback which challenges even their most cherished beliefs. This Tai-Chi sense of balance enables people to lead without demanding that events always move in their preferred directions.

The industrial-era leader tried to mold events to achieve his or her personal vision. Our new leaders are learning that they can only create positive directions by working with other people and with environmental realities.

We must learn to create together. Continuance of current competitive models will ensure the end of the world in the not too distant future. The proposition that the human race will either grow up or blow up is absolutely true today.

Those of us who want to be leaders must therefore examine how we react to the polarities of the balance statement above. Do we find it most difficult to recognize that everything we do is critically important? Or have we failed to understand that we can all too easily be wrong and that the dangers of error are compounded when we do not listen to feedback? Some who claim to be leaders live by the first belief and forget the second. All too many who should be leaders are paralyzed by the full understanding of the second statement and see no evidence which would cause them to live by the first.

The most effective leadership styles for our current conditions are still largely invisible to our cultures. There are hundreds of thousands of servant leaders in the United States but their contribution is typically ignored or trivialized. We need to link them so that we can mesh our efforts and their skills.   OOO

If You Know For Certain that You're Right, You'll Inevitably be Wrong

I have borrowed this statement from the work of Ruben Nelson, a Canadian futurist, who has been one of the more interesting writers about the implications of fundamental change over the past fifteen years. He develops the implications of his argument at two levels.

First, we must not assume that there are slick and tidy answers to the questions we confront. We must therefore beware of the person who tells others exactly what to do and is always sure how to act. Individuals of this type are still living in the industrial-era objective universe; they have not realized that uncertainty is *inevitable* in the rapids of change.

But there is also a second challenge in this statement that may be less obvious and more difficult to accept. If you are *absolutely* sure of what you are doing in a particular area, it is almost certain that you are closed to new input.

We will only be committed to a single way of acting if we have not yet broken out of industrial-era styles. I remember all too clearly the outrage which developed in the mid-sixties when I stopped making conventional speeches; i.e., telling people what I was going to tell them, telling them, and then telling people what I had told them. People felt that I was irresponsible; indeed, several people suggested that I should not be paid because I had not done my "job." I, on the contrary, realized that I was going in the right direction but was very unsure where it was taking me.

What are the areas where you are unable to tolerate disagreement or dissent? When do you demand that people agree with you? These are the points at which you need to struggle. The one intolerable behavior pattern in the emerging era is intolerance. This whole book is based on the belief that it is necessary to make your choices within a religious or spiritual or humanistic or golden-rule set of values. How else can we help people internalize their highest nature?

If we act as though "we" have the right answers and "they" have the wrong ones, we shall inevitably enhance conflict and violence. If we join in a search for the causes of the conflict and understand that both sides always feel they are in the right, then we may find the possibility hidden within the problem.

The world appears to be in a cycle of rising intolerance. More and more people refuse to understand why other groups and countries feel constrained to act as they do. Nevertheless, hidden beneath the obvious breakdowns, there are positive dynamics. We can nurture them if we work with people rather than against them.   OOO

Do What You Can
Plus Ten Percent for Risk

Human beings grow by taking risks. The feedback from their activities teaches them where they have succeeded and when they have failed. In fact, risk taking is a vital part of growth.

The individual who does not take risks dies. We all know people, even young people, who have decided that life holds nothing more than they have already experienced. These individuals have, in a very real sense, given up, although they may continue to "live" for many more years. We also know older citizens whose physical bodies may be failing them but who continue to be endlessly interested in new developments. In the future, life may be defined as the ability to grow and help others to grow, and death will be seen as occurring when individuals can no longer rise to challenges.

People need to learn to take intelligent risks, however. The universe does not forgive if an individual ignores its laws. A culture which allows itself to decay will not be saved because it was unaware of its dangers.

We grow from our mistakes but we must avoid catastrophic failure. The suggestion that one should do what one can plus ten percent for risk makes this point in a catchy style.

All too often, people and groups in Western cultures either do nothing, or they suddenly try to accomplish everything at once. Growth and change in any field or area is almost always a slow process. We need to start with the skills that we have, use them as well as we can, watch the patterns which emerge and then see where we can be most effective in terms of next steps. The assumption that some people or groups are overnight successes emerges because we do not know the long apprenticeships they have normally served.

When we develop the skills to live with appropriate risk taking, we discover the meaning of the biblical statement, "Take no thought for the morrow." This does not mean that the Lord will provide regardless of what we do. It does mean that if we behave responsibly, we will find a way into the future which makes sense.

I have been greatly helped by the saying, "Life can only be lived forwards, but unfortunately it can only be understood backwards." We are pulled into the future by potentials if we are willing to remain alert to the world in which we live. It is for this reason that being open is ultimately a survival skill.

Individuals who learn the skills of leadership and acceptance have a special quality. St. Francis of Assisi knew these skills in the Middle Ages, for example, as did Thomas Merton in modern times. The vital quality of balance exists in all our spiritual traditions: it needs to be revived rather than invented.   OOO

Freedom and Responsibility

We *must* have an open society which operates on the values of honesty, responsibility, humility, and love. We must also accept the inevitability of mystery—the fact that it is impossible ever to understand a situation completely. It is appropriate to *demand* that individuals and societies accept these preconditions for survival because these conclusions have been reached by great spiritual leaders throughout the world over millennia, and this same set of ideas is now being confirmed by modern secular thinkers using very different language.

The acceptance of this one basic constraint on behavior then provides total freedom for people to think and act as they believe appropriate. Fundamental religious and spiritual values do not provide a single way of looking at the world but rather require each one of us to struggle to enhance the quality of life on the planet.

We need to develop policies which are life enhancing in terms of the realities of today's world. The nature of these policies will continue to change as realities change. For example, the doctrine of a just war has been outdated by nuclear weaponry. Our traditional views of life and death are challenged by the ever growing abilities of doctors to preserve body functions.

The old statement, "I may not agree with a word you say, but I shall defend to the death your right to say it," stems from the recognition of the need for open dialogue. We need at this moment in our history to be reminded once again of the potential for positive change which emerges when people seek jointly for the truth.

This traditional statement is no longer enough, however. It has been used all too often in recent years to justify self-seeking arguments which an individual *knows* to be untrue. We must support the right of people to their own honest points of view. We must challenge those who believe that they have the right to distort the debate to serve their own purposes.

This problem cannot be resolved directly because no one can be sure if other people are telling the truth *as they see it,* or if they are deliberately lying. We can, however, create knowledge systems which decrease the possibility of deliberate distortion and increase the opportunities for honest dialogue. Structures are already developing which can move us in this direction.

Each of us can also commit to never deliberately distorting reality for what appears to be personal or social gain. Lies confuse the search for reality and wisdom in our complex world. We can never tell the truth, the whole truth and nothing but the truth. But we should do the best we can.

OOO

You Can Only Teach People What they Already Know

Marshall McLuhan, one of the sixties gurus, challenged us with his statement that the last way to learn about water would be to ask a fish. Water for a fish simply "is." Living without it would be impossible, and therefore unthinkable.

It is all too easy for us, therefore, to miss critical dynamics which are so obvious they're invisible. Unfortunately, what we don't know can hurt us. Ignorance does not prevent pain or disaster.

In their book *Frogs into Princes*, John Grinder and Richard Bandler show that most psychological breakdowns stem from blocking reality. There are usually escapes from the resulting behavioral traps. But we all too often refuse to see the new approaches and directions which could work for us because they cannot be used until we are willing to cope with change.

The skilled helper of others, whether credentialed or not, enables people to surface what they already know but have not yet faced. Such people create nonjudgmental open space in which ideas can be examined. Previously, these concepts may have been rejected by a person because they were "wrong" or "frightening" or "dangerous" or "unacceptable" or "crazy" or "vague." They may indeed be any, or all, of these things, but a person can never know whether these judgments are correct until the ideas are brought out into the open and examined.

Helpers provide words, images, and concepts for the learner. These clarify muddy and obscure patterns and permit acceptance or rejection of ideas. There are, of course, no tidy patterns; helpers can only do their best using their own subjective and incomplete understandings.

Outsiders can also play similar roles for groups. All long-standing groups develop beliefs and models which need reexamination. Few insiders are willing to take the risk of surfacing new ideas because they fear they may lose their credibility. Outsiders can enable risk taking, but only if their ideas have relevance to the group. Good facilitators uncover new ideas in the group rather than force thoughts upon them.

Helping and facilitating are not dramatic. The changes caused by these processes are slow and sometimes almost imperceptible. But they are not easily reversible. Once a useful idea or model has been learned, people will find confirming evidence for its validity in a wide range of places. It will come to replace the images and visions by which the person has previously lived.

One of my tactics to stay sane has been to make it a rule never to look back less than three to six months when evaluating success. If I stick to my rule, I am often surprised to discover how much progress has been made.   OOO

You Can Either Get Social Change, or You Can Demand Kudos; You Don't Get Both at the Same Time

Have you ever felt frustrated when your words, thoughts, or action plans are quoted back to you without acknowledgment? If you're never affected by this, you have moved further than I in your life-long quest for personal maturity!

Individuals and groups cannot, however, really move with new ideas and models until they have internalized them. Patterns of action and thinking only change when you have moved beyond reflecting about a new insight and have made it part of your perceptual universe.

I remember somebody writing to me about one of my books and saying that she no longer knew what she had learned from the book and what she had known before; this woman had a keen appreciation for the paradoxes of the learning process. Indeed, one truly wise teacher once stated, "If you thank me for teaching you something, you still haven't really learned it!"

The art of facilitating change, therefore, demands that you move beyond your own needs for ego satisfaction and learn to help people recognize the points at which they are ready to grow. The potential for change exists when the ideas and models which people currently use to organize their reality are no longer satisfactory to them. They are then prepared to struggle toward new styles and structures.

There is a widespread tendency to equate the situation in the eighties with that of the fifties. I am often told when I go on campuses that students are apathetic. Apathetic people see no reason to change because the world in which they live seems satisfactory to them. This *was* the situation in the fifties when social structures seemed appropriate to most of the population even though reformers found them dangerous and destructive. So the first step toward change in the sixties was to challenge these structures, so that people would "see" what was wrong about segregation and the Vietnam war.

Today, on the contrary, students and adults are already frustrated, baffled, and angry, and therefore ready to listen to those who propose new directions. We no longer need to stir people up; rather, we need to show them how to make sense of their lives and believe in their ability to effect change.

But we can only do this successfully if we get out of their way. We do not help people change by forcing them to adopt *our* agendas and *our* priorities. Growth occurs when people are encouraged to pursue their own directions rather than required to accept those imposed by others. We are slowly learning this about our children today, recognizing that the important task is to help them gain a sense of their self worth as they are growing up. Unfortunately, we have not yet applied this understanding to adults in most relationships.   OOO

Speak Truth to the Listener

One constant challenge to my style comes because I set out the truth in a way which appeals to my audience. I am often told this is dishonest.

I find this reaction increasingly difficult to understand. I speak and write because I believe I know something worth communicating. I believe that it is, therefore, my responsibility to make my points so they are perceived.

If I consciously, or unwittingly, trigger negative reactions which prevent me from getting through to people, I see myself as failing. If I talk to management using terms which appeal only to labor unions, I should expect to be ignored. If I make proposals for changes in ways which can be stereotyped as right-wing or left-wing, my challenges will be less effective.

My difficulties with those who challenge this style of presentation go even deeper. The criticism suggests that "Robert Theobald" is a single faceted individual. An assumption is being made that I can, and should, come across in the same way to everybody. I reject this view. How I am seen inevitably results from a complex mix of my own experience and genetic background, coupled with the patterns of those with whom I am involved. The central issue is how well I can relate to various people, rather than "who I am."

I have deliberately personalized the statements above. Let me suggest you now reread the previous paragraphs applying them to yourself rather than to me so you can see how you feel about these issues.

How we perceive personal maturity is directly relevant here. I believe that the truly great person is at ease with a very wide range of people and groups and can bring out the best in all of them. Such an individual is able to resonate not only with his own class and creed and sex but is truly a "person for all seasons and all people."

Western society sometimes values people with these qualities, but normally only if they are comfortably outside the mainstream of our culture. We need people who can convince rather than coerce. We must develop individuals who can explain new understandings and truths to the widest possible range of individuals, while remaining conscious of their limitations.

Of course, there are no absolute standards to determine what is right and wrong as we choose our words and styles for various audiences. We must judge on the basis of what we know about those to whom we are speaking. All of us have experienced and know more than we can possibly share; we must carefully choose how we use the limited time we have together.   OOO

It All Depends...

I was taught when I was young that there was a right response to every question; the only trick was to find it. Intelligent people were absolutely convinced at this time that we could find specific answers to all problems. The structures of our society reinforced this type of thinking. For example, many of us debated questions when we were growing up. We were supposed to convince ourselves that one side of a question was right or wrong and then argue it heatedly.

One of my debate topics was whether you should tell a person she was dying. For some reason, this issue stuck with me for decades and I continued to struggle with it. Eventually, I found the correct response, but it was not the one I expected. The only appropriate answer is that "it all depends" on the character of the dying person.

I wish I had gone on to learn a broader lesson immediately. I should have recognized that the right answer to all complex questions is: "It all depends." Unfortunately, it took me a few more years to learn this lesson. Once I did, however, I saw the world from a dramatically different viewpoint.

The religious patterns I had been taught in my youth led me to believe that there were neat and tidy answers to all dilemmas. My new understanding that "it all depends" changed my thinking dramatically. I came to understand that the primary element in personal maturity is the ability to apply spiritual values to the many real situations in which we live each day.

There is profound tension between the various types of religious revivals developing in the world. One pattern of religious leadership informs us that we should insist on certain types of behavior and claims that it is our duty to force people to live by a detailed set of norms. Other religious leaders propose that we should apply the religious values of honesty, responsibility, humility, love, and a respect for mystery in our daily lives to discover what to do in each situation.

This last proposition means that the realities which surround us will continuously challenge us. People will often be overloaded but they will never be bored. They will continue to learn all their lives, particularly about the ways they can more effectively help others. As they grow, they will share their skills. The result will be a significant upward spiral in personal and cultural competence.   OOO

Assume a Positive Response

Have you ever watched somebody arguing in favor of a project, using a style and body language showing that this person has already decided that the cause is hopeless? Have you wondered why anybody would bother to make a presentation if they were convinced that the group would reject them? Such a person isn't aware of the need for leaders to be convincing if they are to be effective.

A primary block to positive action is our stereotypes about who will and will not be supportive of change agents and social entrepreneurs. We reject individuals because we see them as "conservative" or "liberal" or "reactionary." We deny their interest because they are from "management" or "labor," or are members of the media, or because they are male or female, or old or young, or white or black, or over-educated or undereducated.

It may be reasonable to hold beliefs about the *statistical* probability of people in certain groups accepting the profound challenges posed by the new directions of our society. I have, however, become only too well aware that individuals do not fit into statistical norms. I've found interest in change everywhere. My discussions across the country have taught me that both the power structure and change agents are deeply split by the same disagreement. Some in each group still live in a sixties world; others see the need for profoundly new directions.

Effective communication is only possible if one approaches an individual, a group, or an audience in the belief that people will hear you. The first task is to establish a rapport with those you are trying to influence because people will block your message until you do so. If you have enough power, you can, of course, force obedience, but people will obey grudgingly and without enthusiasm.

Individuals are often surprised by the wide range of people excited about positive ideas. They can see why they are *personally* interested, but they have assumed that other people or groups are unreachable. I have found that people will get involved if we appeal to their strengths rather than forcing them to fail because of their weaknesses. Depending on how we talk and work with people, we develop their capacities or keep them on a downward spiral.

Our task is to help ourselves and those around us grow. As we do this, we learn how to help others realize their potential. But we can only be effective when we know what our personal strengths really are. It is then easier for us to support ourselves and others in our unique personal journeys through life.   ○○○

The Problem Isn't Money

How often have you heard, "That's an important issue but the money just isn't there?" Such a statement dodges the real issue. Of course, some people and families and organizations have no discretionary resources, but these are the exceptions in the United States. Most institutions make real choices all the time. In these cases, the proper challenge is, "You're not lacking money; what you mean is that the effort does not have a high priority for you."

These two statements have the same consequence: nothing gets done. The first is an excuse, however, while the second issue is real. Budgets can always be changed if there is a sufficient reason and a high enough priority.

How can we bring about change in a stable or declining system? It is relatively easy to introduce new ideas at times when new resources are flowing into organizations. When resources are being reduced, every individual and group will try to hold onto what they already have and also try to take over resources from others to maintain their position.

Given the way organizations currently work, this is intelligent behavior. People must look after themselves without much concern about the consequences for others or the total system. We therefore need new institutional styles.

One way to start the shift is to adopt a model already used in some personal and organizational budgets. A certain percentage is put aside every year for new directions and responses *regardless* of existing priorities. If we truly believe that a system which is not growing is dying, then we have no choice but to find ways to permit positive change even during a time of decline.

The mechanics are quite simple. If the organization has to remain within its current budget for the next year, each division takes a cut of, say, two percent. However urgent the priorities within the existing division or department, the "new directions" money is sacred and is allocated only for the good of the total system.

During times of rapid change, stagnation is fatal. Existing parts of organizations inevitably tend to be wedded to what they are *already* doing, while new energies are more likely to provide the potential for innovation.   OOO

Mistakes are Inevitable

The industrial era developed a legal myth that perfection is possible. Our whole model of liability stems from a growing belief that people can sue for any failure. A good overall record is no longer an effective excuse; it is sometimes not even a mitigating factor.

We have now reached the point where obstetricians have been sued simply because a child is born less than perfect, despite the inevitability of occasional genetic defects. As a result of this pattern of thinking, costs of malpractice insurance have risen dramatically. People are leaving the profession with increasing rapidity.

Why is it so difficult for us to come to grips with the inevitability of mistakes? One significant reason is the different way we see our mistakes and those of others. Many people see their own mistakes as understandable. They are caused by unavoidable circumstances, pressure of time, and other reasonable excuses. The mistakes of other people are often seen as caused by carelessness or even a total lack of concern. These people have themselves at the center of their lives. Other people blame themselves for every mistake they make and tend to excuse others.

Both of these groups miss the point. We should try to avoid mistakes as much as possible. However hard we try, however, mistakes will occur. Indeed, a system which cannot tolerate mistakes cannot grow.

Balancing a desire for perfection with a realization that growth comes from error and failure is one of the challenges of our emerging era. It is undesirable and impossible to prevent all mistakes and errors. Even in our schools, the classroom seldom provides the opportunity to fail creatively. We teach the "right" answer rather than encouraging the experimental one. Instead, we need an educational system which enables people to benefit from failure rather than avoid it.

In the end, our rejection of failure reflects our lack of belief in human beings. We do not act as though healthy people want to grow or help others to grow. So we struggle to create people in our own image, rather than tempt them to explore their own uniquenesses.

But while mistakes are valuable, catastrophic failures are dangerous and potentially disastrous. How can we distinguish between the two? We walk away from a mistake determined to learn. Catastrophic failures cause us to abandon any hope of personal growth and may even be totally destructive.   OOO

Systems Should Not Fail Catastrophically

I am sometimes told that my work is not significant because change only happens in crisis, and that discussion before crises emerge is useless. I respond to this criticism in two ways.

First, let us assume for the moment that this belief is correct. It remains true that the steps taken when crises do develop will depend on the people and ideas in place when action does become possible and necessary, so it is vital to position people so that they will be ready to act at the moment of crisis. New entrants to a system seldom gain influence in the middle of a crisis because the necessary trust for cooperative work cannot be generated rapidly. They therefore need to be in place *before* the crisis emerges.

There is a second, and deeper, question about this perception. The belief that crises are an acceptable way of forcing change will have to be modified as we leave the industrial era. The development of essentially unlimited productive and destructive power means that humanity now has the capacity to eliminate its own habitat and requires that we learn to minimize the risk of catastrophic failure.

We must therefore rethink all existing decision-making models. Such a step is essential because modern weaponry cannot just be seen as one more escalation in potential destructiveness, as is still sometimes suggested. Today it can destroy essentially all life forms. The fact that humankind has been frightened by every major new weapon in the past does not mean that we can shrug off fears that nuclear, chemical, and biological war would destroy the world. There may be doubts about various hypotheses, such as the inevitability of a nuclear winter, but who would care to test what could happen?

The problems which could arise from mankind's destructive powers are fairly easy to describe. The dangers from mankind's growing productive power are far more complex. We do know that we are living off our capital of energy and raw materials; we do *not* know what standard of living can be guaranteed by renewables *after* we have used up the accumulated capital from earth's long geological history.

Certainly, there has already been significant environmental and ecological damage because of past and existing production. Fortunately, we are discovering tools with which to reverse some of the damage. But our positive policies are not moving as fast as the breakdowns, and nobody knows when degradation becomes irreversible or massive climate shifts inevitable.

We need to find ways to act before crises develop. This will be one of the hardest challenges for the American culture to accept, because it often seems to welcome crisis as the easiest, or perhaps the only, way to force decision-making in tough situations.   ○○○

The New Roberts Rules of Order

Have you felt frustrated at meetings when you were trying to make a critical point? Have you been cut off by maneuvers which permitted people to get their way even though it was clearly against the sense of the meeting? *Roberts Rules of Order* and parliamentary procedures are based on the assumption that people are not open to persuasion. Societies and groups therefore accept the tyranny of the majority over the minority. This pattern could be tolerated when our survival was not at stake, but it is no longer adequate when we face the potential of total destruction.

There are alternatives. Quaker styles prove that people can change their minds after thought and reflection. In that tradition, one person takes on the task of trying to discover the sense of the meeting and helping people to find uncoerced agreement. John Woolman used this patient process over many years and led the Quakers to abandon slavery long before any other American group even considered such a direction.

Recognizing the capacity for new vision is the first step in breaking out of conflict models. An even more important second step, which we are only now beginning to understand, is setting up styles which enable people to manage diversity. It is not necessary for everybody to reach the same conclusion or to behave in the same way. People can use the same space and time to do different things which seem satisfactory to each of them.

We can only benefit from diversity if people are willing to be honest, loving, responsible, and humble. If good behavior must be forced by police power, then there must inevitably be one law for all. (Nevertheless, the application of the law will still be more favorable for the rich and the powerful than for the poor and the weak.)

Because there will always be some people who are unwilling to behave responsibly, and because police power ensures the tyranny of the majority over the minority, we can only benefit from diversity if there is responsible peer pressure. The doctor who misbehaves should be disciplined by his colleagues rather than protected in the fear that the public will see all doctors as irresponsible. (It will, of course, always be difficult to distinguish between irresponsible behavior and creative risk-taking.)

Can people reach the required level of maturity to support new decision-making styles? Nobody knows. However, we must try because we cannot afford to maintain current systems.   OOO

The Need for Open Space

We now know a good deal about how the human mind is structured. But we can only bring about the urgently required alterations in thought and action if we use this knowledge intelligently. The amounts of information and stimuli in the world are so great that we inevitably limit what we perceive. Each of us has our own methods for doing this. We read certain newspapers and magazines but not others;

we go to a few places for vacations and do not explore the extraordinary range of other possibilities; we take on a particular career path and seldom look at other options. Once we have set our directions, they are reinforced each time we act in the same way.

We can think about paths through the brain in the same way as we think about paths in a meadow or forest. The more often a path is used, the clearer the path becomes and the more likely it is that it will be used again. If, however, we choose to move in another direction, the former path will eventually be covered over. The longer a path has existed, the less likely it is to be abandoned. Some roads in Europe were built along trails started before the dawn of history.

It is not only our personal lives which are dominated by patterns. Each group, community, and nation learns to interpret events within a particular framework. We then tend to reject events and ideas which do not fit within our current conceptions. Direct attacks on these frameworks reinforce our prejudices rather than weaken them.

Given the need to rethink patterns and frameworks, we must use what we know about the processes of change more effectively. The first step in supporting change is to give people clear evidence that they are not required to behave in the ways which are traditional in particular situations. For example, we all know how to behave in meetings or how to listen to speeches. We are placed in tidy rows and we are meant to follow conventional styles. People will only feel able to be creative if we change meeting styles and rearrange space.

The purpose of "open space" and "common ground" activities is to enable people to say what they really believe and also to learn to act more effectively. People need to leave the responsibilities of their roles and positions behind when they enter open space, speaking as honestly as they can about their real beliefs. This does not mean that union and management people will agree; it does mean that they will speak out of their guts rather than from the propaganda positions which have developed over decades. Honest conflict within open space conditions supports creativity.

We need to develop a willingness to say what we really believe. Knowledge is not an objective reality which can be found by private study. It is discovered through sharing, and realizing that one's own vision will be partial and that others have much to offer.   OOO

SECTION *6*

Managers of Crisis

Up to this point in human history, profound shifts in cultures have always been forced by massive breakdowns. But, given the destructive power available to us, global conflict is now far too dangerous to be a possible route for change.

On the other hand, it is too late to avoid serious crises. Our past unwillingness to face problems before they have become acute ensures that we will encounter many rocks as we pass down the rapids of change. We can hope to avoid global catastrophe; we cannot hope to eliminate continuing shocks.

How can we avoid total destruction? We must learn to manage emerging crises before they become too severe and compound each other. We can only do this successfully if we take the time to understand the realities which surround us.

The most likely near-term breakdown is economic. This section describes the three options open to us: forcing the maintenance of current models while worsening long-term dangers; permitting an immediate catastrophe, believing that this will minimize long-run pain and suffering; or buying time through intelligent adaptation so that we can move through the breakdowns without falling into global collapse.

Triggers for Change

There are two requirements for effective, large-scale change. First, we need change agents and social entrepreneurs who know how to dream and implement. Effective innovation is "ten percent inspiration and ninety percent perspiration." Second, we need to encourage people to listen to information that helps make sense of their lives even while disrupting past thinking.

The historical record shows that cultures confronted with the need for profound shifts tend to fail. Arnold Toynbee, a great British historian, pointed out that there are many more dead cultures than live ones. The traditional response to current discontinuities would be for a new country to seize world leadership; Western domination would be replaced by control from another part of the world, for example, Asia.

This pattern of shifting dominance may, of course, still occur over decades. But it certainly cannot develop using the traditional mechanisms of war and violence. The invention of nuclear, biological, and chemical weapons has made full-scale wars obsolete as the method of shifting power from one nation to another.

Some clear-eyed people believe that the United States is still the best hope to be the leader of positive change. They see America as the best opportunity but also recognize that it could be an enormous threat.

How then can we move beyond war? One can argue that we have, in one sense, *already* done so. The level of tensions between the communist and capitalist worlds has been so great at various times since the end of World War II that it would have led to war *if it had not been for modern weapons*. In one sense modern weapons are "peacemakers," however much we may hate the logic of this statement.

Most of our concerns about war concentrate on East-West conflict. In reality, the possibility of a holocaust resulting from the growing unrest between the haves and the have-nots of the world is the greatest threat today. All the rich countries, whether East or West, share a common interest in stability. They have done well. The destruction caused by war seems increasingly senseless to them. The poor countries, however, have little to lose. Their helplessness and lack of resources create anger and this anger triggers terrorism. The clash of these two attitudes is clearly apparent as Western countries try to cope with Arab countries that support terrorism as a way of gaining leverage over events.

Western countries do not want to admit that terrorism is a form of warfare. It is, nevertheless, acceptable to those people and countries who feel that other groups or nations are behaving so outrageously that they need to be destroyed but cannot be attacked through a full-scale war. We should remember that both war and terrorism dehumanize. Actions that would be condemned in times of peace are seen as necessary, even laudable, when carried out by terrorists or by soldiers during times of war.

Terrorism is, of course, opposed by the rich countries because it is a major threat to their systems and to the fragile balance in the world today. The open societies of the West are very vulnerable to terrorism. Power, water, transportation, and computer systems are all easily open to terrorist attack. Even more frighteningly, nuclear terrorism has been technologically feasible for years and is the nightmare of those who deal with breakdown scenarios. Another profoundly threatening possibility is disruption based on chemical or biological toxins.

The difficulty in abolishing both terrorism and war is compounded because the production of weapons is currently vital to the West's economy, particularly that of America. A dramatic reduction in production for war would bring on a slump. Indeed, one of the profound paradoxes of our time is that terrorists would not be able to buy weapons so easily if it were not for excess military production in the very nations they threaten.

The stability of the world's economy depends, in current conditions, on continued growth in economic demand. As supply has risen throughout the world, the "battle" for markets has intensified. In some ways, the Third World War is going on now and it is being fought with terrorism, limited warfare and economic weapons. More and more people fear that this global conflict could create a catastrophe in the near future.

We shall only develop the necessary new directions if we recognize fully that the current drive for maximum economic growth is as obsolete as war. The ecological structures of our planet are already showing signs of stress and possible breakdown. The rich countries must learn to share with the poor. In addition, rich individuals must limit their wealth so that the gap between the well off and the deprived within countries becomes appropriate to emerging new realities. We can no longer encourage great wealth in the hope that it will trickle down to those without resources.

The dangers of nuclear holocaust and economic depression are probable triggers for major rethinking. Other elements will enter into our overall change process, and we can anticipate additional crises as we shift from a medical to a health model and from being taught to ingurgitate and regurgitate information to learning to learn on a life-long basis.

Our growing discontinuities provide us with many opportunities to challenge individuals, institutions and cultures to look at change in new ways. We all need to be aware of possible crises so we can use them to create the opportunities for building new directions. In a sense, change agents are managers of crisis. They draw attention to problems and possibilities when people seem ready to deal with them intelligently and positively.   OOO

Shortcuts to the Compassionate Era

During the forty years since the end of World War II, it has been an article of faith with most Western development economists that the poor countries would do best if they followed the route pioneered by capitalism in the nineteenth century. Communist theorists, on the other hand, have pushed for the adoption of their strategies.

The analysis being advanced by Western development economists took specific shape in the sixties as discussions started about the shape of the post-industrial era. W. W. Rostow published a book called *The Stages of Economic Growth* which argued that the developing countries could only reach a desirable post-industrial society by first moving through industrial conditions.

The book was highly influential, despite the fact that both historians and economists disputed the validity of its theories, and even its facts. Nevertheless, its thesis was widely adopted, perhaps because it provided an apparent justification for seeing the poor countries as backward and in need of the inventions, models and ideas of the countries already developed.

The failure of this approach to development has emerged in several ways. The most obvious has been that the gap between the rich countries and most poor nations has grown in recent decades. Few developing nations are catching up with the rich but rather falling ever further behind. There is increasing evidence that they will continue to do so as long as we maintain the current socioeconomic and political order. This overall negative situation has been disguised by the sensational successes of a few nations such as Japan, Taiwan, Singapore, and more recently South Korea.

In addition, patterns of foreign aid and foreign trade can now be seen to have done at least as much harm as good. Many poor countries which were self-sufficient in food, and even exporters of it, now have to import grains. The indigenous economy has weakened as the trade economy has developed.

A classic science fiction story about aid takes place far in the future. Earth has defeated two other planetary systems. One begs for aid and receives it. Twenty years later the economic system has been revived but the cultural mainspring has been broken. Fifty years later the negative consequences are plain for all to see. The other planet refuses aid. The short-run results are tragic. But the need for the citizens of this world to use their resources to recover by themselves brings an extraordinary scientific and societal renaissance.

This story suggest a further problem with foreign aid practices. The shift from agricultural to post-industrial systems will not follow the same trajectory as the shift from agriculture to industry. There is growing evidence that we shall need very different success criteria for the compassionate era.

This suggests that we should draw out the implications of development in a very different way. Let's look at the implications of Figure 1 on the next page. If the approach suggested here is correct, it is possible to move directly from the agricultural era to the compassionate era without adopting the patterns of the industrial world. It suggests further that the sixties images of the post-industrial era are invalid.

Is there any reason to believe that the shortcut approach proposed here will be more successful than the suggestion that developing nations should use capitalist or communist routes into the future?

One reason we should take this possibility seriously emerges from the work of Arnold Toynbee, a British historian who studied the rise and fall of cultures. He showed that each cultural epoch usually had different leadership because

Fig. 1: Shortcuts to the Compassionate Era

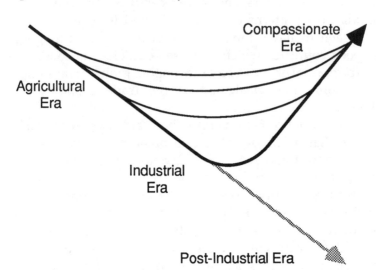

those who were successful in one period often had difficulty in managing the transition into the next one. This pattern certainly exists today. The power centers of the Western world are clearly the least willing to deal with the problems and opportunities of our changing world.

However, the diversity now emerging within countries makes it unwise to rely on simplistic analogies. Some parts of Western nations are already responding to a totally different rhythm as compared to the power centers. Work I have done in the Heartland of America over recent years confirms the fundamental difference in attitudes between the heartland states in America and the two coasts.

People in the central states have a deep sense that they have been left behind and that they will not catch up by parroting the techniques and models now being used to create growth on the coasts. They may be the ones who are ready for the new styles of leadership needed in the compassionate era. Underdeveloped parts of European nations such as the Basque area in Spain and the Highlands and Islands of Scotland are also challenging the conventional wisdom.

We must learn our way into the compassionate era. This book has set out some of the elements, but the specifics for each group and nation will be unique. Change will only be successful if it is based on the strengths of each person, group, and country.

This is the developmental challenge of our time. One technique to achieve this goal has been developed in Nebraska. We have created a convincing image of the state for the year 2000 and have explored its implications for families and groups. This image is being critiqued and will serve to inspire action by both citizens and leaders. Its role at the State level is similar to the way in which a strategic plan is used within a business. Up to the current time, most state planning efforts have set up conflicting scenarios which confused the public and made effective planning impossible. This new technique opens up space for effective discussion and the development of new directions.   OOO

Patterns of Stress

A few people became convinced in the early sixties that continuation of current trends would lead to disaster. An image I used at this time was of people sitting in the club car of a train and getting quietly drunk. From time to time, they looked out of the window finding they were moving dangerously fast. Nobody, however, got up to find out why. If they had, they would have discovered that the train engineer was dead and the throttle was stuck fully open.

The question that emerged was how to move off the current set of tracks. In the early seventies, I drew the figure below (Fig. 2). The train was on track A speeding toward line B which was a cliff over which we would fall if we did not wake up to the dangers of our situation. Point C was a new positive vision. The necessary task was to discover desirable images for our new world which people could accept.

Fig. 2: The Runaway Train in the 1960s

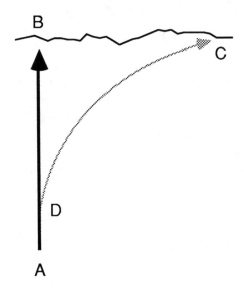

Many people have tried to share new visions with the American people in the past. One of the more dramatic, and successful, examples resulted from Edward Bellamy's book *Looking Backward* published in 1888. Clubs sprang up all over the country to discuss his hopes and prophecies. His death undercut the movement but the book remains influential even today.

Having a vision is inadequate by itself, however. Communicating this vision effectively is the further challenge. It is far easier for people committed to one set of policies and directions to incorrectly hear challenges, than to accept the need for rethinking. Change agents must have high communication skills which maximize the mesh between the needs of those who are listening and the potentials of the new vision. Change in the sixties took place at point D where social entrepreneurs helped people change their thinking.

I had forgotten this diagram until quite recently when I was trying to help people see the realities of the current moment in time. I started off by drawing my diagram in the same way as I had in the seventies. I rapidly recognized our current reality could be more usefully represented as in Figure 3.

Fig. 3: The Runaway Train in the 1980s

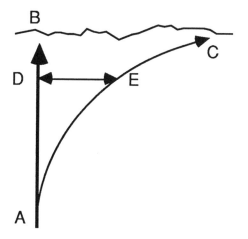

I realized that many people in our culture had indeed begun to move away from industrial era approaches in the mid-1960s. Confirmation of this reality is available in *New Rules*, written by Daniel Yankelovitch on the basis of extensive polling. He showed that many of the fringe attitudes of the sixties have been accepted by a large percentage of those in the 1980s mainstream.

The line DE suggests our position in the mid-1980s. A few people still totally committed to industrial-era styles, values, and epistemologies are at point D. The sparseness of their numbers is hidden by the fact that industrial-era rhetoric is still dominant among those who move public information in the culture: academics, politicians and the media. These groups are still largely unaware how much the general public has changed.

This does not mean, however, that many people have moved to point E—indeed it is highly doubtful if anybody is fully aware of all the implications of our new era. People are strung out all the way along the line DE. To make matters even more complex, individuals will often have changed their views on one topic but not on another. One could imagine, for example, parents who see the need for learning-to-learn but who still favor a punitive prison system. Or people who favor promotive health but still believe that the poor are totally responsible for their problems.

Severe conflicts around these issues are developing within our global system, countries, communities, groups, families, and individuals. You can think of the line DE as a rubber band which is being stretched more and more thinly. Eventually it will snap. Shall we create the potentials of our new era or be pulled back into a destructive attempt to preserve the past?

Some people believe that there is no doubt about the answer to this question, arguing we shall inevitably make the positive transition. Others, including myself, do not agree, believing the outcome depends on our levels of commitment. *Rapids* argues that it is our joint responsibility to help individuals, families, groups, communities, institutions, states, nations, and the global community bring the new world into existence.

Most people and groups of people are now aware that old patterns are not working. They will, however, fall back into them if they are not shown alternatives. Communication of these alternatives requires, in turn, that we do not baffle and frighten people more than they already are, but rather invite them to join with others on an exciting and positive journey.

Fortunately, we are now at the point where we can show the process of breakdown, and also the ways in which we can rebuild cultures if we should choose to do so. We shall first consider economic cycles, and then generalize what we learn.   OOO

The Long-run Economic Cycle

A consistent pattern in industrial-era societies has been approximately fifty to sixty-year, long-run economic cycles. Half of each period has shown sustained upward dynamics, and the other half has seen continuing downward pressure. These cycles were first described by the Russian economist, Kondratieff. More recently, Jay Forrester, a systems analyst at the Massachusetts Institute of Technology, has used computer programs to show why this pattern develops.

Many people are aware of this long-run cycle because of memories of the Great Depression of the thirties. Images from this period are in people's minds, either because they lived through the period or because they have seen movies or heard their parents' or grandparents' memories about these hardship years. The horror and the pain are still fresh.

Unfortunately, the patterns and risks of a deflationary spiral have been largely forgotten by the emerging generation of policy-makers, who have come to believe that "it cannot happen again." These people talk about built-in stabilizers, social safety-nets, and worldwide commitments. They argue that we have learned our lesson and that we will not permit a depression to develop. The harsh reality, however, is that we do not yet know how to avoid the consequences of our past actions.

Why do long-run cycles occur? The process is really quite simple. We can start our analysis from the point where there is too much supply compared to demand. Firms are no longer willing to buy more equipment; people no longer have the resources to increase their consumption; banks are overextended in terms of the loans they have handed out when they believed that the good times were going to roll forever.

A long-run downward spiral now begins to develop. People and firms draw in their horns when they find out that conditions are getting worse. This causes more people and firms to cut back and the process snowballs. Because there are no strong sectors of demand, nothing can stop a continuing decline for many years. Indeed, the very steps various players take to preserve their own positions make things worse.

This is particularly obvious with protectionist pressures. The problems start when countries lose production and jobs to overseas suppliers. This causes business, labor, and politicians to band together to try to stop imports. As each country imposes restraints on others, those who lose ground retaliate in order to protect themselves. Export demand declines still further.

The end result of this process in the thirties was war because the levels of tension which developed through protectionism led to profound anger and hatred, eventually erupting in violence. Most historians directly relate World War II to the frustrations of the Great Depression. Industrial protectionism is growing again in the eighties, coupled with a new and frightening pattern. Countries with extensive agricultural sectors are using government controls to reduce prices so sharply that everybody is suffering severely.

In the past, wars increased demand, of course, and brought the economy out of slumps. Consumers are ready to purchase because they have been short of money during the depression. After the Second World War, there was also a baby-boom which further increased the demand for production that was still inadequate. At this time in long-run cycles, there appears to be no limit to what can be produced profitably. Increases in production and consumption continue and everybody appears to benefit. Standards of living grow and it looks as though the good times will go on forever.

Eventually, excesses emerge. People and firms want more than is available, and inflation develops. During the most recent long-run economic cycle, the period of rapidly growing demand coincided with the Vietnam War. President Johnson tried to deliver both guns and butter so the economy became over stretched. Prices rose increasingly rapidly. The two oil shocks of the seventies worsened the state of the economy dramatically, and inflation became a major threat.

Toward the end of the seventies, people began to adapt, believing that inflation would continue forever. However, to the surprise of almost everybody, President Reagan tamed inflation during his first years in office. Rates of inflation have dropped and continue to stay very low.

This development should have been anticipated, however. The underlying reality of the eighties is deflationary rather than inflationary. The current downward pressure on prices could easily get out of control. The parallels between the end of the twenties and the mid-1980s are substantial. The economy is weak in many sectors: there is already a farm depression, an overwhelming surplus of shipping, and far too much office space built on the basis of unrealistic depreciation allowances. In addition, consumers have been provided with excessive amounts of credit and are overextended.

Even more serious is the overwhelming debt crisis. Far more money has been loaned to the poor countries than can ever be paid back. Only an acceptance that this money is gone for good can prevent the financial collapse of many of the developing countries. Finally, most of the rich countries are running massive government deficits. They are increasing the amount which citizens have to pay each year to service the national debt.

What are the options? We can continue to pour credit

into the economy, trying to put off the evil day when a depression starts. We can accept that a depression is inevitable and permit it to develop, hoping that we can contain the worst of its dangers. Or we can find a novel way to work out of our current crises.   OOO

Option One:
Continue to be Credit Junkies

The economic expansion of the last ten years has been based on continual increases in credit. Governments have gone further and further into debt, a pattern unprecedented outside of war periods. Consumers have been offered the opportunity to extend their credit far beyond their realistic capacity. Foreign governments, particularly developing countries, have taken on obligations which most analysts believe will never be repaid.

How did we get into this situation? Inadequate consumption has been the major block to economic growth at least since the beginning of the twentieth century—except during times of war and their aftermath. The primary need has been to find ways to enable people, firms, institutions, and governments to buy.

The problem of too few buyers worsens at the end of each 50-year cycle. The drive to keep up demand becomes more frantic. Risks are taken in extending credit which would not have been considered in saner times. In addition, prosperity has been in place for so long that the possibility of any major collapse in the economy is largely ignored.

Several special factors have complicated today's situation. One was the oil shocks of the seventies. OPEC countries made so much money that they returned it to western banks for lending. The large banks, flush with funds, handed out money, promising clients they could not lose. At that time it was true, as real interest rates were low and sometimes even negative because the rate of inflation was higher than the cost of borrowing.

The balloon burst in the recession of 1980-82. Inflation tumbled; interest rates fell much more slowly. Real interest rates which had been negative turned around and became unusually high.

Three groups of borrowers have been particularly hard-hit by their seventies' borrowing. The poor countries needed money to pay for the higher cost of oil so they could continue to achieve high rates of economic growth. Today, the debts of many developing countries are overwhelming. They have been forced by the International Monetary Fund to reduce their standard of living in order to pay off the banks. The potential for internal insurrection caused by this hardship is all too clear.

Another problem area is the agricultural sector of the economy. Farmers were told by government, academics, and bankers that they should plant fence-row to fence-row in order to meet the needs of the poor countries of the world. They also were informed that they could not lose money because the value of land would continue to rise and so would the price they could gain for their products. Many farmers went heavily into debt to benefit from the promised bonanza. A depression has since developed in the rural areas of the country. Land values have plummeted; excellent acreage in Iowa and Nebraska now fetches less than half, or even a third, of what it did five years ago.

A third area of major concern are the oil firms hard hit by an almost totally unexpected drop in fuel prices. This has been the last straw for many banks in the American states and Canadian provinces dependent on energy extraction.

Oil firms, the poor countries, and rural areas now find it very difficult to get bank credit. Indeed, the amount of credit available to all troubled borrowers has declined dramatically. Nevertheless, the economy has been propped up by four primary policies. First, excessive depreciation allowances for commercial building in an early Reagan budget have kept construction expenditures up. This has resulted in the building of huge excesses of office space. Vacancy rates in a number of cities are at 25 percent or above, particularly in Texas cities hard-hit by the oil-slump. It is widely believed that rates of office construction will fall by as much as 50-75 percent in some cities over coming years.

Second, consumers have been encouraged to keep on buying by the extension of credit cards and other loan facilities. Of course, this strategy will eventually be very costly as more and more people default on their debts. The implications of more lenient bankruptcy laws on the viability of our overall system may be far more serious than is currently understood.

Third, banks have been willing to lend money for all sorts of activities connected with mergers; financing has been conducted through "junk bonds" whose strength has not been tested in any sort of recession. The stability of the banking system itself is in grave doubt—the number of problem banks suffering severe stress has grown even outside the depressed agricultural and oil states.

Finally, the governments of most countries were prepared, until recently, to run large federal government deficits. This has pumped up demand but only at the cost of still further increasing interest payments which must be met in the long run by raising taxes.

The excesses described in these four paragraphs may or may not stop in the immediate future. People are increasingly worried about all of these patterns—most particularly federal deficits. The extension of credit will eventually be controlled; the only question is when.

The hard reality is that the longer we avoid dealing with today's fundamental imbalances, the harder the task will become. We are putting bandages on cancers and thus ensuring that the chances of an eventual cure are decreased.   OOO

Option Two:
An Eighties Great Depression

When I was cutting my intellectual teeth in the forties and early fifties at Cambridge University in England, the primary fear of economists was that we would see the emergence of another thirties depression in the near future. This seemed strange to me at the time. Now we can be clear why it was ridiculous.

Demand for goods and services—and money to buy them—had accumulated during the war. The problem of the forties and fifties was therefore a shortage of supply rather than a shortage of demand. The failure to see this reality caused some serious errors in policy-making.

The forties and fifties errors emerged because we all tend to perceive the dynamics of the recent past and forget longer-run patterns. We are making similar mistakes today. Behavior in the eighties is still being controlled by the fear of inflation that was the key problem of the seventies. While inflation does still exist in some of the poor countries, particularly the Latin American nations, the rich countries are in a very different situation. Deflation and a slump are quite possible.

Recessions have sometimes been created deliberately. The evidence shows that this was the case in the early eighties, when the Reagan Administration aimed to squeeze inflation out of the system through a recession. The process was successful, although the cost was higher than intended and also greater than many competent people believe was necessary.

On the other hand, no one would deliberately create a depression or slump. There is general agreement throughout the world that they would be profoundly dangerous both within and between nations. Nevertheless, the patterns currently developing and the policies being proposed throughout the world, particularly the drive toward protectionism, could create what nobody wants.

There is far more supply in the world than people can pay for. This does not mean that there is more than is wanted. Many people are starving in the poor countries and there is serious poverty in the rich, so changes in the distribution of rights to resources could balance supply and demand. But there is currently little sign of any major shifts in income distribution strategies which would benefit the poor.

If we continue to fail to balance supply and demand, we shall eventually slide into a slump. It is often argued that slumps will not develop because policymakers are committed to avoiding such a result. This thesis is not convincing today, however. While there is no reason to doubt the will of the international community to avoid such a catastrophic development, there is every reason to doubt their competence. The world economy is now interconnected in ways nobody understands. National control is also increasingly ineffective.

What would be the result of a world depression? Countries which were unable to find enough jobs for their workers would try to keep jobs at home by protecting national industries. They would forget that the losses from such policies will be greater than the gains because other countries will inevitably retaliate. Protectionism develops because it appears to result in short-run gains. We are already moving rapidly along this path.

The consequences are all too predictable. Within countries, there will be more and more unrest when there are insufficient jobs for the labor force. It is estimated that growth rates in the five to six percent range are required just to keep up with the young workers entering the labor force in the poor countries. Failure to attain this level of growth will produce a rootless and angry class. A slump coming on top of past downward pressures by the International Monetary Fund could be catastrophic.

There was a surprising willingness to endure the hardships of the thirties. Most people believed that government was doing the best it could. Few observers think that today's citizens would be so understanding, so the likelihood of severe violence would be very great. One can, indeed, see the beginnings of this danger as extreme groups are finding it possible to recruit those who are losing faith in the intelligence of government, and perhaps more seriously, its commitment to caring for the problems of people.

The most serious dangers would, of course, emerge through clashes between nation-states. Everybody knows at one level that war is now intolerably dangerous and must be avoided at all costs. But the anger which would emerge in a slump could erode the barriers to armed conflict as the rich countries react to the terrorism which will inevitably worsen if a slump occurs.

More and more conventional analysts fear the possibility of a slump. Even conservative economists and papers are arguing that we must provide additional credit to prevent this danger. But additional credit would imply that current budget deficits and trade imbalances must be perpetuated.

This seems to many to be the only possible step because they believe we must avoid a major slump at all costs for the reasons given in this section. Is there any way out of this apparently insoluble double bind?   OOO

Realistic Options

Today, three primary economic options are currently recognized:
• One would hold off an economic slump by injecting more and more credit into the system; this would worsen the eventual problems;
• The second would withdraw the current forced feeding of the economy and bring on a major slump. The costs of this route are very high, and possibly terminal;

• A third group argues we have already been through the difficult period, and the economy has settled down. *Fortune* magazine claimed in the summer of 1986 we could look forward to a long period of remarkably steady growth.

All of these three possibilities are unrealistic. Therefore, we must develop a fourth option by buying time so we can break out of our whirling dervish economy dependent on compulsive consumption. We need to prevent the development of an overall and massive crisis by breaking it up into smaller, more manageable issues. We can do this only if we accept that maximum economic growth is no longer a viable policy and that we need to move in new directions.

We need to move toward optimum growth policies which raise the quality of life. Commitment to this goal will change our statistical measures and our beliefs about the meaning of success. Such a shift in fundamental strategies will challenge all our current assumptions and force dramatic changes in the conventional wisdom.

Fortunately, we can already identify a number of new directions as we start to define the meaning of optimum growth:

• Our excessive debt loads must be reduced in ways that are as equitable as possible and also minimize the risk of bringing on a worldwide depression;

• The rate of growth in population should be decreased as rapidly as possible;

• Economic systems and strategies that encourage or force waste are intolerable;

• Costs of pollution must be borne by those who create them and not dumped on the society in general; and

• People must be given opportunities to break out of starvation in the poor countries and poverty in the rich; limits will be needed on excessive wealth.

A watershed in our thinking will come when we abandon the belief that we can only be saved by achieving a high enough economic growth rate. When we realize the necessity for this dramatic break in thinking we will regain power over our culture and society. We overcame the thirties slump by finding new ways to encourage consumption. The questions we must now resolve in order to chart a positive course into the future are far more complex.

We must consider, first, the possibility that the world will run out of land, water, energy, and raw materials. This was one of the primary warnings of *The Limits to Growth* report of the Club of Rome. Economists challenged the conclusions of the report arguing that there could always be substitution for those factors of production which were in short supply and that the operation of the market would prevent the serious consequences predicted by the analysis.

The Club of Rome's report was indeed vulnerable at many points. But the issues raised will not go away. Sooner or later the earth will have to live on its stock of renewable resources rather than on the capital of materials and energy laid down over geological time. Ignoring this reality is irresponsible. We can escape it only by arguing that new technologies will always save us or that space travel will bring us what we need. Are these beliefs realistic? Can we afford to count on them as a certainty?

There is a second far more troubling and more immediate issue. How much pollution can the environment absorb without irreversible damage? This question was also raised by the Club of Rome report. The responses so far developed are unconvincing because they do not go to the heart of the ecological questions we face. We do not have an accurate model of the world ecological system. Indeed there is a real question whether it is possible to build such a model. Nobody can be sure what the consequence of massive pollution will be.

Surprisingly, there is general agreement that the earth had a period of remarkably stable and benign climate during the twentieth century but that this stability is probably breaking down. The effect of human activity on our planet earth is now significant enough to change local ecosystems severely and to require intelligent decision-making about the limits which need to be placed on human habitation and behaviors. Living as I do in the Southwest desert, I am deeply disturbed that we are building toward an ecological catastrophe resulting from lack of water, worsening air quality and a micro climate caused by the trapped hot air of cities in the desert.

We also know that there have been large scale climate shifts in the past, causing the development of ice ages. We do not know what triggered these changes, although there are a growing number of theories about the possible causes—most of them mutually contradictory. There is more and more concern about major shifts in climate patterns as early as the 1990s or the first decade of the twenty-first century. Some predict rapid global warming, and others a new ice age.

Fortunately, we do not need to understand all the issues before taking the first vital step. Our economic system is currently set up so that any potential increase in production must be matched by consumption unless we are willing to accept unemployment. Now is an excellent time to change our system so we can make societal decisions about production, consumption, work, and resource distribution rather than be constrained by the ability of technology to increase productivity. We need to build a culture fit for complex, concerned, loving human beings to live in.   OOO

Avoiding Catastrophic Failures

The long-run cycles in Western industrial systems have played a critical part in ensuring the continued viability of rich societies. They have purged the excesses which accumulated as oversupply built up. Obsolete goods and factories were consigned to the dustheap. Of course, this unemotional description of a slump hides the agony of people who were made useless. It also enables us to forget the wars that have been fought for markets. Nevertheless, the mechanism did work, despite the pain it caused.

Today, however, we must learn how to prevent slumps and other massive catastrophes because the potential consequences are too dangerous. To do this we must gain a better understanding of what goes on during the development of the long-run cycle.

Economies emerge from a slump in a state of relative balance. (See Fig. 4, below.) People have been sufficiently frightened by the disasters they have experienced that they choose to be careful. But as the years go by, excitement grows and the magnitude of short-run cycles begins to increase. Constraints, both regulatory and within professions, are imposed. But the general trend remains upward, and over excitement takes hold. Governments try to control these excesses. But trends still look good to people. At this point, systems move onto a very dangerous downward slope through feverishness controlled by ever increasing power and then into chaos.

Fig. 4: The Economic Cycle

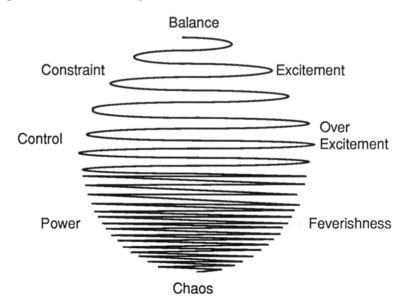

At the end of the Carter administration, we were firmly set on the course through fever into chaos because of excessive demand and inflation. The Reagan administration controlled inflation, but has been willing to allow other imbalances by pushing huge amounts of credit into the system, and by allowing business funding through junk bonds. Other countries have followed similar policies.

Can we move back up the circle and reverse the normal direction of flow toward entropy and breakdown? This question arises not only for economic slumps but also in human breakdowns. We can learn how we might act economically if we look at personal patterns. We used to assume that alcoholics and drug users had to fall, literally and figuratively, into the gutter before they would be willing to save themselves. It was thought that they would not be willing to make the effort to escape their cravings until there was absolutely no other option. We have now discovered ways to surround the alcoholic with family, friends and colleagues and to challenge him or her into accepting the need for change. This is a tough role because the alcoholic has perfected avoidance mechanisms and escape hatches just to avoid facing the ultimate consequences of his or her path. But an individual can be effectively confronted and the approaches to make the challenge as successful as possible have been developed over time.

Similarly, we have learned better skills for preventing catastrophic breakup in marriages if people wish to avoid anger and hatred. Families can be counselled in ways which help them decide whether they can effectively get back together or need to break up. If breaking up is necessary this can also be handled positively, although the need for legal processes all too often destroys this possibility. Similar processes have been developed for larger groups including institutional renewal. I was able to help a community college in Dallas rediscover the excitement of teaching and the joy of education. We do know the patterns and understandings which are required for both personal and institutional renewal.

We need to develop large-scale social processes similar to those which have been learned for individuals, families, and groups. We should confront people with the need for change in ways they cannot easily avoid. Personal change is achieved by forcing people to listen to what they don't want to hear. It might seem then that all we have to do is send more and more messages about the growing evidence of potential catastrophe. This will not work, however, because most people have become experts at tuning out messages they don't want to hear.

Unpleasant messages are all too easily blocked unless the messenger is trusted. The alcoholic eventually listens because the costs of ignoring the challenges of family, friends, and colleagues is too high to be tolerable. We must develop a trust relationship with those we want to influence in the society if we hope to get them to listen and then commit to avoiding total breakdown.

People are so stressed today that the first step toward trust is to give them a chance to unwind. This is a fundamentally different strategy from that usually chosen by change agents. *Rapids* is one step toward this new approach. It starts from the assumption that we can challenge people to move toward an attitude of realistic hope. Most people no longer believe that there is a shortcut to a better world, but many are still willing to try to build new approaches with each other.

The core aspect of our work will be to pull individuals, groups and systems away from the chaos into which we are drifting and back toward balance. Fortunately, a great deal of imaginative work has already been done in this area. We have tools and models that can be employed, once we fully understand our directions and why they are fundamentally different from those of industrial systems.   OOO

SECTION 7

Putting It All Together

The purpose of Rapids is for you, the reader, to develop new skills and models which help you in your thinking and action. The process of application starts with this section of the book.

I cannot provide you with rules of thumb or gimmicks. I can show you how to apply Rapid's styles to your personal and social situations and introduce you to the many groups with whom you can journey further.

The choices you and I make in the next few years will determine whether our children and grandchildren will enjoy a high quality of life. I hope you will decide to put your energy behind building a more humane culture.

If you do, you will not only be creating a better future but opening yourself to passion, compassion, love, and joy. The route we need to take is not easy but it is the only one worthy of us.

The Importance of Context

The Rapids of Change has been about the importance of "context" in making decisions. I have been showing that the world has changed so dramatically that we must look at new realities and use new styles when determining what to do.

It is not easy to grasp exactly what the meaning of the word "context" is. Let me start from an issue which is a commonplace one for those of us who live in Arizona. Dry streams and rivers are good places to ride under normal conditions because the going is far easier than around cactus and mesquite. But if thunderstorms are around, one must stay out of dry washes because floods may rush down them very suddenly. People who ignore this danger may well be drowned.

The context in this case is the weather which is not under human control. Let us look now at a couple who are under increasing tension because their marriage does not seem to be working. They live in one context so long as they remain committed to the marriage; they enter another one when they decide on a divorce. And the context in which the divorce takes place will vary depending on whether it is a "friendly" or an "unfriendly" one. Each of these human contexts has its own rules and styles: partly defined by the couple, partly by the expectations of others, and partly by the social structures of the culture which will determine what behavior is feasible and what is not.

In addition, the human systems within which we make decisions change over time. The message of *Rapids* is that the shifts are taking place at an enormously increased rate. As these shifts take place, the rules of the game alter. For example, the advantages and disadvantages of a divorce are profoundly different today than they were at the beginnning of the century when it still led to widespread ostracism.

This is the fundamental meaning of the aphorism "it all depends" in Section 5. People only make effective sense of their lives as they become skilled in determining the context in which they are operating. The message of this book is that many of the traditional contexts have already been destroy- ed. Nevertheless, we continue to act as though old patterns are still dominant even though they are no longer the way in which most people live. For example, the predominant image of the American family is husband, wife and two children: in fact, only a small minority of people live in this way.

Politics are also conducted in contexts derived from past experience. The context for much political decision-making until very recently was the desire to avoid another thirties- style depression; this was challenged in the eighties by the desire to prevent inflation. International politics in the fort- ies through the sixties was largely controlled by the belief that there should be "No more Munichs"—the agreement which gave Hitler's aggression the green light. In the seventies and eighties one of the dominant contexts has been "No more Vietnams." Lying behind all these percep- tions is the belief that the world must be structured in win- lose terms and that we cannot all benefit from any possible agreement.

Today's primary problems emerge because we continue to operate out of obsolete contexts. We do this personally, in families, in nation-states, and globally. The challenge we therefore confront is the conscious creation of contexts which are relevant to our times.

At some levels, of course, this is not a new issue. Throughout history, people have had to partially define the way they saw the world. However, the freedom of most people was radically constrained by the expectations of their peers and of the overall social system. One true novelty of the late twentieth century is that "everything has come loose" and most people have to make a far wider range of choices than ever before. The need to deal with diversity and uncertainty has therefore grown enormously.

And the issues have become more complex. I recently made a presentation to legislators and others in the State of Washington on ways to think effectively about the issue of nuclear waste. As with other issues, dealing seriously with nuclear waste means we have to deal seriously with our attitudes toward economic growth and war. The social entrepreneur takes a risk when he raises questions of reforming a group's context because this approach may prove unacceptable when it requires people to look at a broader range of issues that will probably complicate their task. Therefore, I was pleasantly surprised when the general reaction of the legislators was favorable; it confirms my belief that people are indeed ready to operate out of a larger context.   Learning this skill will give you a valuable tool.

In many cases the blocks to looking at the broader picture are primarily conceptual. The closer one comes to one's individual belief structures, the harder it is to step back and see what is blocking one's effectiveness. Few of us are really aware of the belief structure out of which we operate and the booby traps which we have developed for ourselves because of the way that we have learned to think about the world. *Rapids* has shown that the type of behavior one needs to be an effective leader is very different at the individual, family, community, bioregional and national level.

The Rapids of Change is an initial attempt to help people deal with the diversity, complexity, and uncertainty on different levels, using a variety of tools. The remainder of this book provides various opportunities for coming to grips with your area of concern by using two very powerful tools:

• Reforming the context of a question so that a very specific issue becomes enlarged to a level where people can make real choices rather than pretending to be in effective control; and

• Extending your power by identifying groups already working as social entrepreneurs in your area(s) of interest. Many of these groups are described in the Appendices.   OOO

Discovering the Relevant Question

Following is the text from a speech I made to the Washington State Legislature on the issue of nuclear waste disposal. I did not advocate any particular position on this issue; rather I wished to define the contexts which would affect the legislature's decision-making. I suggest that you use this as an example of the "thinking-through" process. It is designed to help decision-makers and others avoid the trap of reducing a major issue to a narrow personal or political perspective.

My presentation followed several panels which presented two radically different approaches. One argued that it was possible to analyze nuclear waste issues using currently available tools. The other stated that all of our tools were powerless to cope with issues that spanned tens of thousands of years and might make large areas dangerous for life. I started my presentation by making it clear that I very much agreed with the second group.

People are now well aware of the need for fundamental alterations in directions. However, they do not know how to come to grips with the overall patterns which are shifting the landscape in which we live. Creative leadership is needed if the current inchoate pattern of concern is to be translated into an effective search for profoundly different directions. My object today is to stimulate you to be excited by the most extraordinary moment human beings have ever experienced. We are being forced to move beyond war and compulsive consumption to a culture based on ecological sanity and compassionate caring.

As all of you who work in politics know, a search for a new answer or policy response emerges from a perceived imbalance in the current situation. One or more people see that "something needs to be done." The reason for the activity may be to find benefits or it may be to avoid dangers but there will always be a perceived need for change.

Our brains move down accustomed pathways and force new data into old pigeonholes. Scientists ignore new material which does not fit their models. Groups try to maintain their modes of operation even in the light of overwhelming evidence that they are not working. Breaking out of this inertia requires a strong awareness of either possibilities or dangers.

Once an imbalance has been understood, activity starts which aims to break out of the problem or to take advantage of the possibility. In our industrial-era culture our attention usually goes toward solving the problem as it has originally been defined, rather than looking at what the deeper issue may be. This is true at the individual level as well as at the group level.

In formal bureaucratic systems, this tendency occurs in its formalized perfection. A group is asked to study a certain question. When issues are raised which do not fit within the guidelines, they are shoved aside because it would be inappropriate, and often even "dangerous," to challenge the task as it has been laid down by higher authority.

This is the issue I shall examine today. We need to break out of our current pattern of finding super-sophisticated answers to super-obsolete questions. We need new types of groups which concentrate on *defining* today's relevant questions. Fortunately tools are now available for this type of work.

Let me now make three specific points before I go further. First, we must be fully aware that the habit of looking for answers is deep in our whole culture and backed by the patterns and indeed the epistemology of our industrial-era system. There is no quick fix to break out of this pattern.

Second, there are groups which are already trying to be effective in doing the new type of work which I believe is necessary. In your own work in the Washington state government and at the Institute for Public Policy at Evergreen State College is evidence of the desire people have to break out of current patterns. I am also impressed by the graduate work on system theory going on at Antioch University in Seattle and the programs which have been developed by the Northwest Regional Foundation in Spokane and also Future Spokane.

Third, I shall be talking about ideas and patterns which are already emergent in the current culture, rather than theoretical ideas which may or may not come to fruition. Some state or region of the country is going to recognize that building new knowledge systems is the leading edge of the culture, and the geographical area which supports this work is going to benefit greatly. I should stress that this does not mean fixing the *current* model. It means devising a system which fits our fundamentally new realities and moves towards new patterns in incremental steps.

The Nuclear Issue

The dangers posed by nuclear waste are, as we have heard again and again this morning, unparalleled in human history. We are bequeathing to many generations a danger against which they must guard. None of our technologies, nor even our levels of consciousness, equip us to deal with the challenges we took upon ourselves when we entered the nuclear era.

Under these circumstances there is a natural tendency to try to close Pandora's box and to put back all the secondary, tertiary, and other consequences of our total commitment to win the Second World War. The Greeks were not successful in their task and neither will we be. Even if we should decide to shut down all nuclear activity on the most rapid time scale possible without unacceptable disruption, we face a massive task of disposing of the wastes which already exist.

Large-scale nuclear wastes have already been created and we have to deal with them. This will remain true regardless of future decisions. It is true, of course, that if we should decide to get rid of all nuclear technologies in the near future the problem would be closed-ended. It would then be possible to find a finite solution which would be the least risky and the most easily managed. More probably, however, we shall continue to be involved in the disposal problem for many decades.

The problem we face is all too clear. We are making choices for future generations. We are taking risks which may not be manageable. The dilemma we need to take seriously is that all the choices we can now make are profoundly risky and that there are no easy potentials any more. We are co-creators of our universe and we cannot be sure how we should move.

Before we choose any specific response, we must therefore ask whether we have really posed the right question. Nuclear wastes are only one reason why people want to get rid of nuclear technology. The more pervasive issue is, of course, the fear of nuclear war. Many believe that the only proper course is to achieve total nuclear disarmament. Indeed, some of the recent Soviet-American negotiations suggest that this is no longer totally a pipe-dream.

What would happen if this should occur? We must come to grips with the reality that we would simply replace one balance of terror with another. The fear of nuclear weapons has turned our attention away from the dangers of biological and chemical weaponry. These are just as destructive and far cheaper. So long as countries fear each other, they are not going to disarm. Military efforts will simply be displaced from one area to another. And even if nuclear arms were all destroyed, the danger of their being rebuilt would continue to exist.

Nuclear weaponry and wastes are indeed profoundly dangerous. But we shall never come to grips with their implications until we recognize that they are part of an overall change which has altered the nature of the globe on which we live. Our survival now depends on our ability to cope with the complexity and the dangers of the world we have brought into existence. This issue is broader than nuclear wastes and must be tackled before we can look at whether our societies want to maintain or to abandon nuclear technologies.

The Abolition of War and Violence

It is profoundly unpopular to admit that nuclear weapons are "peacemakers." For many this is an Orwellian phrase. But who would deny that Russia and the West would have gone to war at one or more times during the last forty years if the dangers of mutual destruction had not been so high? Modern weaponry has made war infeasible between those powers which have access to it.

War, of course, continues on the rest of the globe: it is easy for those in the West to forget how many conflicts are going on at this time. Admittedly, much of the warfare is part of the global struggle between two apparently incompatible worldwide philosophies. But the fact remains that war has become infeasible as a method of settling major international disputes because no side dares to raise the stakes so high that the other is driven to the wall and massively uses nuclear, biological, and chemical weaponry.

We live in a strange world in which we pretend we are fighting according to the old rules, but we are actually engaged in a weird, tragic, and unacceptable form of communication. The United States could have won the Vietnam war if it had used its nuclear armament but this was seen as too dangerous. Many lives were lost until the morale of the United States gave out. The Soviet's situation in Afghanistan is similar.

We must eliminate warfare if we want to survive. But this means that we must change the total global system to manage conflict in new ways. Wars have been the technique by which conflicts have been resolved, since the nation-state came into existence. The great French diplomat, Clemenceau recognized this when he said, "War is the continuation of diplomacy by other means." We are forced to ask what must happen now that major war is infeasible. We have to look at new methods of settling conflicts which will not involve violence.

The elimination of violence between nations cannot be an isolated change, however. We shall be forced to alter all our methods of dealing with conflict at every level of our society. I sometimes fear that neighborhoods would use nuclear weapons to resolve their disputes if only this destructive power was available to them. The task before us is to discover ways in which conflict can be used to spark creativity and to discover the potentials which could be achieved by meshing different perceptions of reality.

We change our minds when other people and groups, operating out of different perceptions, are able to show that there is an alternative reality. Thus the more we can be open to varied viewpoints, the less likely it is that we shall be blindsided by patterns which we have failed to perceive.

This is the first of the huge shifts which is being forced on the human race at this point in time. We have grown from a time when "our" tribe was good and "theirs" was bad, through a time when "our" city was good and "their" city was bad, to the now declining industrial era when "our" nation was good and "theirs" was bad. We are currently moving beyond nation-state politics.

At one end of the scale we are moving to a world where more and more decisions can only be taken on a global scale and where global integration is necessary. The need for worldwide systems such as climate information, telecommunications, and disease control is now so crucial that they continue even while armed conflict is being waged. This interconnectedness will grow.

At the other end of the scale, we are moving down to local decision-making in the community and the bioregion.

There is more and more demand for people to have control of their own destiny in areas such as schooling, economic development, and libraries rather than being controlled by outside laws.

This is shifting the responsibilities of state governments dramatically. On the one hand, states are being forced to act in ways which were largely national in the past. This is seen most clearly in the growing relationships between states and sovereign nations, particularly in the field of development. Washington State's role would increase dramatically if it would understand the full potential of the Pacific Rim and take leadership in this area. The world is learning to look West rather than East. On the other hand, state government should be less involved in making decisions for communities and more active in helping each community define its own questions and decide what it wants to do. We should no longer force behavior on others but rather encourage intelligent decision-making in the light of changing realities and contexts.

The End of Maximum Growth Strategies

The challenge of ending violence is indeed a difficult one, but almost everybody is aware that nuclear war is an infeasible strategy. In addition, many people are aware of the dangers of nuclear wastes resulting from both commercial and military nuclear technologies. There is therefore a constituency for the discussion of these issues. It is far harder to discover people who are looking at the need for fundamental rethinking of our current commitment to maximum economic growth.

Once again we must start this discussion from the issue of nuclear power. In the United States, nuclear power is an important but not huge element in supplying required electric energy. Some nuclear power advocates argue that electric generating capacity will be in short supply in the nineties in North America. But I would assume that many current estimates of growth are likely to be too high because the United States is not going to be competitive in the production of many heavy goods in the coming years and because industry estimates of economic and energy growth have already been too high for many years. Nevertheless, the chance of getting rid of nuclear power in the United States in any short time is certainly low; getting rid of all nuclear energy in the world is impossible without very great disruption. France, for example, has essentially gambled its future on the viability of nuclear power.

Supposing, however, that there was a worldwide decision to eliminate nuclear power. There are then only two major routes which can be used to deal with the gap. The first is to employ other energy sources: either oil, gas and coal, or renewables. The second is to cut back on the energy that is needed both through increased efficiency and through lowered production and consumption.

Let's start with the most obvious option for our culture. If we don't use nuclear power, then we will try to use more oil, gas, and coal. Despite the current glut, there is overwhelming evidence that oil production in the United States has peaked and that we shall be moved back into a shortage of supply by the beginning of the twenty-first century. Indeed, oil imports climbed significantly in 1986.

This means that if we use a reasonable time-frame for planning, our fossil fuel will increasingly be coal. Coal is a dirty and dangerous fuel to mine and the cost in lives lost and damaged through ill-health is high. Nevertheless, while safety is a critical issue, it is not the overwhelming question that needs to be considered.

The long-run wildcard, which we are paying far too little attention to as a society, is the potential for massive climate changes. The amount of CO_2 in the atmosphere has dramatically increased and many scientists warn that a greenhouse effect is developing which is significantly warming the earth's surface. If this is true, there will be major changes in all coastal areas. They will be more dramatic on the East Coast because of its flatness, but the West Coast will also be affected.

Climatologists agree that there are signs of massive climate "instability"—that the relatively stable patterns we have enjoyed through the first half of the twentieth century are breaking down. In addition, more and more people seem to be assuming that it will be necessary to limit CO_2 emissions and at the same time to reforest the earth as the major way to absorb excess CO_2. Given that coal is a major contributor to increasing CO_2 levels, there are obviously grave problems in replacing nuclear power with coal over the long haul.

If fossil fuels are not viable, then what about renewables? There is one pragmatic problem and one longer-run issue. The pragmatic problem is that the developmental costs of renewables, like solar and hydroelectric, are not attractive when compared to current low energy prices. Only if our culture became convinced that major shortages and problems awaited us in the future might it be willing to pay the high development costs today.

The second problem is that renewables require a profound change in the way we think about our relationship with nature. Instead of being available whenever and wherever we wish, the use of renewable energy resources requires cooperation with the ecological system. The sun has to shine for solar energy to be effective, and the wind has to blow for windmills to operate. Use of vegetation for biomass also depends on the seasonal cycle. The use of renewables moves us away from a world of control into one of collaboration with natural systems.

Thus a decision to turn to renewables would necessarily be part of a larger shift. Our society has so far tried to gain more and more control and be less and less interdependent with nature. This model is now totally obsolete. We are therefore forced to look at an alternative world where we reintegrate ourselves—both in terms of working with each other and of working with the environment.

There is one last possibility for avoiding this massive need to rethink. Could we increase efficiency enough to be able to do more with less while keeping our other systems of thought and action essentially intact? There is still a long way to go to produce optimum energy efficiency in the world; waste is still particularly high in the United States. But the gains from efficiency are finite while the requirements of a continued maximum growth strategy are limitless.

We must develop a new vision if we want to survive. The key question today is what does this new vision look like and what steps do we need to take as we seek to discover and apply it?

The New Vision

A critical first step is to replace the current worldwide dependence on maximum growth policies with a commitment to a high quality of life and environmental balance. This would mean that we would cease to make maximum growth our central preoccupation.

The central problem of our industrial-era system is that we are on a tiger from which we dare not dismount. There are both internal and external elements to the pressures which require us to commit to maximum growth strategies. Internally, our systems depend on the maintenance of full employment. This is the way people get income, a sense of purpose, a place in life, and dignity. While safety nets are still in place for those without jobs, they have been considerably reduced in scope throughout the world and particularly in the United States. Given that the way to reduce unemployment is to increase production, we must force up consumption so as to balance our productive capabilities and keep the number of jobs increasing as fast as people need them.

Externally, we have created such massive debt structures that the only hope the poor countries have of meeting their interest payments—let alone ensuring the repayment of capital—depends on substantial growth in production. In recent years, however, the gross national product in many of the poor countries has declined because of the austerity imposed by the International Monetary Fund. Only a major increase in the size of the world's economy can prevent default so long as current systems remain in place. Indeed, there are many analysts who admit that default has already effectively developed but we continue to paper over the ever growing cracks.

To make things worse, there is a close tie between the internal and the external problems. When unemployment levels are high, there are strong pressures toward protectionism. Those industries which are losing sales try to influence government to limit imports from other countries. The only factors which have prevented this threat from causing a world slump are the feedback loops which ensure that protectionism imposed by one country results in retaliation by another, as well as the commitment of the Reagan administration to stand firm against protectionist legislation. But there is little doubt that the volume of trade will be decreased if current inadequate levels of employment persist and if policymakers continue to be committed to current socioeconomic structures.

It is long past time that we recognized that the maximum growth models of the industrial era are destructive in the new era we are entering. More and more of the public understand and are supportive of the need for environmental protection. A growing proportion of the population expect more from their lives than a job and leisure—there is a drive for meaningful work and a happy family life.

A New Course for Washington State

Washington State would benefit if legislators judged policies from the viewpoint of whether they:

1) Provided a high quality of life for its citizens;

2) Maintained the environment of the Northwest bioregion, the nation, and the world for the long-run future; and

3) Provided people with the opportunity to make intelligent decisions at all levels particularly individual, community, the Northwest bioregion, and the globe.

The choice of this direction by Washington State would explicitly recognize that the tools and models it has used up to the current time are no longer valid. Decision-makers would re-examine their economic policies including the costs of recruiting firms from outside the state. They would include in their calculations the need for new attitudes toward bio-regional commissions including those which stretch across the Canadian border. They would recognize that Washington is part of the Pacific Rim and would develop a very different spatial perception recognizing that distance is being eliminated by computers and satellites.

In addition, policymakers would look at specific shifts in various policies:

• They would examine how to shift education from ingurgitation/regurgitation to learning to learn on a life-long basis;

• They would examine how to move from an emphasis on medicine to an emphasis on promotive health;

• They would examine the implications on lifecycles of an aging population as well as the other driving forces of our time;

• They would discover how to produce a justice system which protected the population rather than being organized around the needs of the courts, the police, and the criminals;

• They would rethink the ways in which the unfortunate can be helped without forcing them into a position of dependency;

• They would redefine work in a time when computers will take over repetitive tasks; and

• They would recognize that differential access to knowledge is going to be the source of many social ills.

The state that chooses to take on these challenges will leap-frog over current problems and grasp the insurmountable opportunities of the future.

The Implications for the Nuclear Waste Question

I'm sure that many of you feel that I have gotten so far away from the subject of nuclear waste that I cannot pull myself back. I, on the contrary, believe that I have provided the context in which any useful discussion of nuclear waste must take place.

I would suggest to you that there are two different possible futures and that the way one looks at nuclear wastes is different for each one of them.

1. Let us suppose that we decide to stick with maximum growth policies. In this case we shall generate all sorts of wastes which are highly dangerous and toxic. The problems of nuclear wastes will be acute but they will only be part of the issue of how we continue to manage our waste materials. Indeed, some of those dealing with chemical wastes would argue that this problem is more critical than that of nuclear wastes. The evidence about the increase in birth defects in the United States, apparently associated with chemical hot-spots, is chilling and is one of the most under-reported stories in the United States.

I reject this future as a viable one.

2. The alternative future is the one that I proposed earlier. In this future we recognize that toxic wastes of all sorts are highly dangerous but that they cannot be managed unless we commit to balancing economic growth with ecological realities to ensure a continuing high quality of life. This then becomes one theme of the next election. The other critical themes would examine how we move from a culture in which conflict creates violence to one where it supports creativity.

I am aware that we have not yet thought about the policy measures required to manage this transition from the current dynamics to the sustainable future in any serious way. While we can define directions, we have not yet discovered what our specific strategies should be in many cases. But the commitment of state legislatures could clarify these issues rapidly.

To be effective, however, we need to understand the limiting factor in our planning. It is not the one to which we normally pay most attention. It is not energy. It is not the environment. It is not wastes. It is not production. It is not consumption. *The key issue is the ability of human beings to cope with the change which is taking place all around them and then to enhance their capacity to act intelligently.* We have to find a way to manage rapid change without massive breakdowns. The human race is capable of madness if it loses touch with reality. There is a clear danger of wide-spread individual and social insanity if we continue to be unable to make sense of our world. The growth of extreme right-wing groups is one of the symptoms of this possibility.

Our most critical task is to help people understand the broader issues. It is not difficult to design a suitable process for all interested citizens of a state. I would challenge the executive, the legislative and the judicial branches as well as public, private and voluntary sector organizations to pioneer in developing the new systems and patterns required to help all students, whether in school or out, to come to grips with our changing realities.

In the last two years I have worked in Nebraska on these issues, particularly with state government. I found an extraordinary hunger for dealing with fundamental issues. People are ready to be challenged. Are we ready to create the necessary structures? OOO

Choosing Your Next Steps

This book has necessarily been aimed at many types of people with a wide range of concerns and passions. The whole message of *Rapids* is that we must honor the diversity of people. The remainder of this book therefore suggests many different ways in which you can continue your journey toward greater understanding of the context in which we currently live.

However, each of us faces the same key task. We need to understand more fully our own personal contexts so that we can be more effective in our choices. Nobody can make our decisions for us. Each of us has to determine for ourselves what we want to do and what will be beneficial for us.

Indeed, many of us need to go back a further step and examine why we choose to remain stuck in situations which are obviously self-destructive or destructive of our relationships. It is now known to psychologists that many individuals, families and groups are committed to preserving their negative behaviors and that they sabotage themselves when they see signs that things are getting better. We not only need to look for the ways we can be most effective but we must also watch for the warning signs which suggest that we are not truly committed to a more effective and creative life-style.

I have struggled for an image to convey the options which you can find in the following Appendices. Think of *Rapids* as the lobby of a building where exciting discussions and actions are taking place. The lobby has been decorated so that many different types of people can be comfortable in it. Imagine that the lobby in which you are sitting has a number of doors...

The *first door* opens onto a long corridor and there are a number of rooms leading off it. The rooms have a bewildering range of styles and furniture. But each one of them is designed by people who are trying to create one or more of the changes which are required as we move into our new era. Some of the rooms are tidy and organized, some are cluttered, some are completed and well-designed, some are obviously being redecorated. Some of them have good climate control while others seem much too hot or cold.

These rooms have been created by various organizations and periodicals which aim to provide opportunities for people to think and act in the rapids of change. Appendix A provides a listing of a number of organizations which share the basic beliefs set out in *Rapids*; we hope you will choose to get involved with some of them. You can browse through this list and decide which organization will be most helpful to you at this point in your life. Because most of these groups are short of resources we do ask you to write to a limited number of groups which you think may be directly useful rather than send a form letter to everybody.

Compiling this list was not easy. First, there is a huge number of positive groups. To avoid overload, the number of groups listed was limited; the omission of a group does not mean that it is less valuable or useful. If your group would like to be considered for listing in the next edition, let us know.

Second, since most of the readers for this edition live in North America, few resources are listed outside this area. Let us stress that this does not mean that North America is the only area interested in bringing about this type of change. When the book is published in other parts of the world, we shall produce a regional listing of social entrepreneurs.

Finally, we have tried to choose organizations which appear to be reasonably stable and committed to their tasks. We make no guarantees, of course; you must choose where you want to put your effort. We are finding improved ways to communicate between groups which have so far concentrated mainly on one particular aspect of the overall task, and are just beginning to examine means of effective quality control. Naturally, each person will benefit from a different experience and the message of this book is that you must find it for yourself with a little help from your friends. So you need to explore the various rooms along the corridor and enter those that appeal to you personally.

Appendix C gives additional information about one particular room behind the first door. This area is of great interest to me because I have put a great deal of my effort into it over the last twenty years. In addition, it is the room where a great deal of the drafting and redrafting of *Rapids* took place. This is the room in which *Action Linkage*—the oldest general purpose networking organization in the United States and possibly the world—meets. Action Linkage, or AL, was designed to help people deal with the concerns expressed by this book.

Action Linkage is an open space which is committed to enabling people to realize their dreams and visions. It is designed to encourage passionate discussion. This non-organization attracts people who want to be on the frontiers and are interested in how to be effective leaders. The characteristics of the Action Linkage room are often hard for people to grasp. If you read science fiction, you can think of it as a space which keeps on shifting: every time you think you have it tied down, it moves again. But, paradoxically, it *is* a defined space with a set of structures and a relatively defined purpose.

Action Linkage members generally agree with the arguments of *The Rapids of Change*. Much of the current work is in terms of designing rooms where sub-groups can talk effectively about how to enlarge and develop the arguments in *Rapids*. Obviously each section of the book is absurdly limited and there is a need for extension and development of the thinking. Task groups on health and education already exist, and others are being developed for development and justice.

The *second door* off the lobby leads to a computer which asks you to state your interests so that the expert system can help you find the groups to which you may want to pay most attention. It assumes you currently know where you want to put your effort. The computer asks for a personal profile and then makes specific suggestions as to what you might read, and what action group you could join. You will enter essentially the same rooms that you would through the first door, but you will get there more directly.

Unfortunately, the design of this computer system is still in process. What is available in Appendix B is a brief listing for each section of *Rapids* that includes periodicals and organizations available to help you pursue your current interests. We must stress again that these are only partial lists and represent our best judgment to date of where to look for resources and activities. Some sections have only a few resources listed which may represent a current lack of concern about these subjects. We would obviously be particularly interested in hearing about materials that should be included in these sections.

Behind the *third door*, you will find a comfortably furnished room with people talking about how to create a world with a high quality of life. There is a lot of passion interrupted by bursts of laughter. People seem to be enjoying themselves despite the seriousness of the subject. From time to time, heated arguments develop but they seem to be an accepted way of learning. If you observe for long enough, you will find that the room enlarges as new groups develop: each group finds its own space which is comfortable for its own needs. In addition, the accoustics are superb so that while people are aware of the presence of other groups in the room, they are able to do their own talking and laughing without disturbing others.

Appendix D will tell you about a study guide which is available to support this sort of discussion. It is designed so friends and colleagues can talk to each other about the implications of *Rapids*. The process is structured so as to create the open space which encourages people to be honest about their concerns and their passions.

This study-guide process is effective for those who want to get a broader view of the world. It is a wonderful way to discover how different people can see the same reality from widely varied perspectives. It is a way to break your stereotypes about the types of reaction that one will get from the old and the young, from labor and business, from church people and educators. I continue to learn that people are different and unique and constantly surprising. Art Linkletter taught us that "kids say the darnedest things." Adults do too when they are given a chance to talk about the issues which challenge them.

There is a *fourth door* off the lobby. Immediately on the other side, there is an opportunity for consultation before proceeding through a pressure gate which contains strong warnings requiring caution.

People who go through this pressure gate scout the nature of the rapids and its direction so others can learn the challenges we face. Primitive and risky vehicles are available which permit people to scout the river and to come back with images and visions which can inspire us as we move ahead. Some artists, some politicians, some social scientists, some media people, and some children enter this space and bring us back knowledge. But it is a lonely and dangerous task and we need to give people the best chance of survival and support we can as they do this work.

There are already a lot of competent but isolated people who are performing this scouting function. It is our hope that this book may help to bring some of them together in ways which will enhance their effectiveness. Appendix E expresses briefly some of the dreams of Knowledge Systems, Inc. which is publishing this book and invites people who are concerned with this sort of activity to contact us.

As I have already said, I cannot make effective choices for you nor do I want to do so. When I am asked what I will not give up as I go into the future, I reply that I cannot abandon my commitment to empowering others. The only hope we have of making the necessary transformations in the time we have available to us is for all of us to become our own heroes and heroines.

I can hope that this book has made you believe that you can start on a journey which will make your life more exciting and more effective. My greatest reward of the last thirty years has been to watch the personal growth made possible when people are challenged to reach their potential. We need a culture of hopeful realism that will challenge and inspire both people and institutions. I hope that *Rapids* will move us in these positive directions.   OOO

Social
Entrepreneurs

The following organizations and publications agree with the basic approach of The Rapids of Change and support its direction. They are committed to the development of a positive value-based culture and support movement toward a quality of life orientation in their thinking and action. You are invited to contact the groups which you believe will be most useful to you in your own personal journey: descriptions have been provided by the groups themselves. Those listed range from the highly theoretical to the very practical.

The breadth and depth of the response from these organizations is very exciting because it clearly reflects a growing sense of the need for cooperation between those concerned with fundamental change issues. We should stress, however, that as is the case with all attempts at linking and networking, there are no guarantees of successful matches. Individuals must choose where their energies can be best used and decide if their levels of energy, commitment, and finances mesh with the efforts of the group.

These organizations specialize in examining various parts of the current change process and are relatively clear on the implications of what is currently happening. The greatest need today is to link these specialized groups with mainstream structures which have the competence and the skills to bring these new ideas to fruition. To mix metaphors, *Rapids* is designed to serve as a bridge between current decision-makers and those groups and people which have been developing the ideas and models we must adopt if we are to survive.

Please do not mail to all organizations on this list but pick those most likely to be of help. Please enclose a self-addressed, stamped envelope when asking for information. The criteria for their selection is given in *Choosing Your Next Steps*, pages 202-203 in Section 7. Information on *Action Linkage* is given in Appendix C.

Animal Town Game Co.
Contact: Ken Kolsbun
P.O. Box 2002
Santa Barbara, CA 93120
(805) 962-8368

We are here to offer you quality products chosen for their usefulness, innovativeness, educational value, durability and/or artistic value—and most important, for the fun you can receive from them. We are a family-owned mail order company which began in 1976 to give people access to cooperative and non-competitive games. We started by inventing and manufacturing boardgames which deal with Mother Nature, social well-being and cooperation. We design each one to be informative and thought-provoking as well. Over the years, we have gradually broadened our line, and now offer a wide selection of quality family-oriented games, playthings, books and cassette tapes.

Association for Humanistic Psychology
325 Ninth Street
San Francisco, CA 94103
(415) 626-2375

The Association for Humanistic Psychology, founded in 1962, is a worldwide network for the development and application of human sciences which recognize our distinctively human qualities and innate potentialities as individuals and members of society. Our goals are to promote humanistic philosophy, introduce humanistic principles into public policy making, and provide our members with excellent opportunities for professional development and personal growth. AHP links, supports and stimulates those who share this humanistic vision of the person in the fields of psychotherapy, holistic health, peace psychology, organizational development and many more. We invite you to join AHP by writing to us at the above address.

Bicycle Network
Contact: John Dowlin
P.O. Box 8194
Philadelphia, PA 19101
(215) 222-1253

The Bicycle Network is a people-to-people, transnational network of bicycle advocates working to strengthen the bicycle's position as a healthful, low cost, energy efficient means of transportation and as an important link between the public and public transit. The Network publishes a quarterly, *Network News*, which is a booklet of news clippings covering all new developments on bicycle transit and pedal technology. It also publishes an annual wall calendar of photos, Cycle & Recycle, celebrating the bicycle as both vehicle and symbol and one of the "rays of hope" in the transition to a post-petroleum world. The Bicycle Network meets annually in New York City in conjunction with the N.Y. Cycle Show (usually Presidents weekend in February). For more details, send a return address label and postage to the Network's address above.

Brain/Mind Bulletin
Editorial:
 P.O. Box 42211
 Los Angeles, CA 90042
Subscriptions:
 P.O. Box 70457
 Pasadena, CA 91107
 (213) 223-2500, (800) 626-4557,
 (800) 233-9228 (in California)

A concise four-page report, edited by *Aquarian Conspiracy* author Marilyn Ferguson and published every three weeks, reporting on current breakthroughs in brain science, psychology, education, learning research, states of consciousness, cultural change and related areas of interest. Yearly subscription is $35. Send SASE for free sample, to editorial address.

Catalyst
Contact: Susan Meeker-
 Lowry
P.O. Box 364
Worcester, VT 05682
(802) 223-7943

Catalyst is a bi-monthly newsletter for those interested in "putting their money where their heart is." The focus is small-scale, decentralized, self-sustaining (both financially and environmentally), cooperative with an awareness of our dependence on each other and the earth. Regular sections on businesses, organizations, land stewardship, reviews, info on alternative investing around the world and a special focus on the Third World (particularly Central America) and Native American issues. Latest info on the "new economy," too. Subscriptions: $25/year, 6 issues.

Center for Nonviolent Communication
Contact: Marshall B.
 Rosenberg
3229 Bordeaux
Sherman, TX 75090
(214) 893-3886

The Center for Nonviolent Communication is an international educational network providing opportunities for people to develop the literacy necessary to respond compassionately. Our workshops can be designed to fit the needs of peace groups, civil rights groups, street gangs, teachers, clergy, law enforcement officers, and public service workers to mention just a few. We support the development of local autonomous groups that pass along our training. Thousands of people participating in our training have expressed appreciation for how they are able to apply what they learn with us in their personal, professional and political activities.

Center for Supportive Community

Contact: Kathleen
   McGuire/Zack Boukydis
186 Hampshire Street
Cambridge, MA 02139
(617) 492-5559

We teach peer counseling (consisting of reflective listening and experiential focusing), consensual decision making, and "third person" conflict resolution. We have an ongoing Sunday night group, open to anyone in the community at large, where these skills are taught. Also, we do training workshops for other organizations. We distribute a manual (*Building Supportive Community: Mutual Self-Help Through Peer Counseling*, Kathleen McGuire) teaching the basic skills. We also consult with people running parenting networks and have developed a manual teaching these skills, *Support for Parents and Infants: A Manual for Par-*

enting *Organizations and Professionals*, C. F. Zachariah Boukydis, Ed., Boston: Routledge & Kegan Paul, 1986.

Center for Urban Education

1135 S.E. Salmon
Portland, OR 97214
(503) 231-1285

The Center for Urban Education (CUE), established in 1968, makes it possible for citizens and community organizations to deal constructively with change by pioneering innovative community services, identifying regional trends, offering resources which encourage personal, professional, and organizational development, and buildingcommunityconsensuson public issues. CUE presently provides services to the community through four major program areas: 1) the Information Technology Institute provides training, technical assistance, and access to a computer lab; 2) the School of Management provides classes on management topics for nonprofit organizations; 3) the Community Resources Program offers a community library, and publishes information for the community including a statewide media guide, and a quarterly journal, *Rain*; 4) the Columbia Willamette Futures Forum continues to explore long-term scenarios.

Chinook Learning Center

Contact: Fritz & Vivienne Hull
P.O. Box 57
Clinton, WA 98236
(206) 321-1884

The Chinook Learning Center, established in 1972, is a non-profit educational center and community located on Whidbey Island, Washington and situated on sixty-four acres of evergreen forest and meadowland. Rustic facilities include a turn-of-the-century Finnish farmhouse, a newer retreat house, two cabins, a cedar log sauna, two gardens and an orchard. Chinook's central purpose is participation in personal and cultural transformation through communion with God and affirmation of the sacredness of all life. It seeks to teach a hopeful vision of human life in harmony with the earth and to call people to live as an interdependent global family.

Choosing Our Future
109 Gilbert Avenue
Menlo Park, CA 94025
(415) 853-0600

Choosing Our Future is a non-partisan and nonprofit organization that is working to revitalize citizen dialogue through Electronic Town Meetings held over television at the local, regional and national level. Power in a democracy depends upon the power to communicate and mobilize public opinion. Electronic Town Meetings offer an effective way for citizens to use television and telephones to add their voices to the climate of public opinion that guides our leaders.

The Churchman/Human Quest
Contact: Edna Ruth Johnson,
  Editor
1074 23rd Avenue, North
St. Petersburg, FL 33704
(813) 894-0097

The Churchman is a uniquely humanistic journal, published nine times a year, with emphasis on integrity in our society leading toward a peaceful, interdependent world community. Authors care about our country's role in international affairs; they care about distortions, disinformation, and false propaganda dissemenated by "false prophets" in today's society, making inroads into people's thinking and politics. Each issue is replete with forthright comment on these concerns.

**Communities, Journal of
  Cooperation**
15 Sun Street
Stelle, IL 60919
(815) 256-2252

Since 1973, *Communities* has been the primary source of information about thousands of intentional communities dedicated to personal growth, community development, and social transformation. *Communities* is a valuable resource for anyone interested in community and group dynamics, family life and relationships, health and well being, work and food cooperatives, innovative educational and technological initiatives, creative problem solving, etc. *Communities* serves both individual and community needs for information exchange, networking, and promotion of the community movement, demonstrating the relevance of intentional community experiences to society through their accomplishments and the broad range of opportunities they provide for accelerated personal, community and social development. A one year subscription (4 issues) is $16. The 1987-88 *Directory of Intentional Communities* (available Spring 1987) is $8.

Connect/US-USSR
4835 Penn Avenue South
Minneapolis, MN 55409
(612) 922-4032

Connect/US-USSR is a Minnesota-based, nonprofit, nonpartisan organization working to foster educational and cultural exchanges between the United States and the Soviet Union. The organization, which grew out of a citizens' initiative, began in 1984 with a children's art exchange. Since, then Connect's programs have expanded to include professional exchanges, the hosting of Soviet visitors, and the facilitation of educational and cultural programs for both adults and children. The purpose of these connections is to educate Americans and Soviets about one another and to build mutually beneficial relationships between the people of the two countries.

Consultants for a Positive Future
Contact: Lois George-Smith
2509 N. Campbell Avenue
Suite 220
Tucson, AZ 85719
(602) 325-6767

Consultants for a Positive Future—consultants, trainers and speakers covering virtually every field of experience—was started in June of 1985 to provide a pool of professionals for meeting the challenges and opportunities of our rapidly changing reality. Through the shared sense of possibility that human beings can create a socially just world based on values fundamental to the world's greatest philosophies and religions and to the founders of this country, we work to promote grassroots planning. Our purpose is to empower clients, to help them discover their unique understandings and abilities, and to help them find the most all-around beneficial solutions at every level—groups, businesses, organizations, and communities.

Co-op America
Contact: Paul Freundlich
2100 M Street, NW, Suite 310
Washington, DC 20063
(202) 872-5307, (800) 424-COOP

Co-op America is a nonprofit, member-controlled, worker-managed association that links socially responsible businesses and consumers in a national network, a new alternative marketplace. Co-op America is bringing together groups and individuals to build a cooperative, socially and environmentally responsible economy; to challenge mainstream assumptions about the necessity for marketplace manipulation and competition; and to encourage people to use their purchasing power in a way that reflects their values. Through Co-op America's semi-annual catalog, you will have access to quality products from all over the Americas made by people whose values are reflected in their products and their workplace. Through Co-op America, you will have access to our cooperatively structured health insurance plan which allows you to choose the services of alternative or traditional practitioners.

Cultural Exchange Service
Contact: Carlos Nagel
240 East Limberlost
Tucson, AZ 85705
(602) 887-1188
Assists in linking individuals in Mexico and the U.S. to accomplish activities that involve both cultures; uses personal relations based on long-term committments involving integrity, trust, good faith, honesty and love; and focuses on education, natural resources in border region, US/Mexico transfer of technology projects that are non-confrontational and cooperative.

Earthstewards Network
Box 10697
Bainbridge Island, WA 98110
The Earthstewards Network is hundreds of active, excited people like you, in the U.S., in Canada, and sprinkled literally all around our planet. Earthstewards are a network of active peacemakers in little towns and in big cities all around the earth, showing by example how to live their global consciousness, and how to resolve conflict in win-win ways. The Network is a support group for those who want to make a positive, peace-filled difference in the world and in their own lives. Earthstewards are people everywhere, connected by a network of communication and consciousness, who know the power of their thoughts and actions and are directing them in loving service.

East Bay Briarpatch Network
Contact: Roger Pritchard
1514 McGee Avenue
Berkeley, CA 94703
(415) 527-5604
The East Bay Briarpatch Network, one of the parts of the Briarpatch Society, is a support network for small socially responsible businesses located in Alameda and Marin Counties. Members are committed to honesty, openness, sharing-exchange, and fun in their businesses and to high-quality contributions to a better society through their businesses. Network support activities include monthly meetings, speakers,

parties, trips, a business clinic, a newsletter and member directory and a network coordinator. For further information: 2 pp Briarpatch Network description $1; *The Briarpatch Book* $5; *Appleseeds Directory* $3 (an annotated list of 40+ successful local Briarpatch type businesses in every sector of the economy). Out-of-area calls are returned collect.

The Elmwood Institute
Contact: Elizabeth Hawk
P.O. Box 5805
Berkeley, CA 94705
(415) 848-1127

The Elmwood Institute was founded to help facilitate the shift from a mechanistic and patriarchal world view to a holistic and ecological view. Its members share the conviction that the final decades of this century must be shaped by an ecological world view if we are to survive. Our social institutions, however, are still tied to an outdated view whose limitations are now producing the multiple manifestations of global crisis. Through small gatherings, conferences, publications, and other projects, the Elmwood Institute hopes to cross-fertilize new ideas, nurture ecological visions, and apply those visions and ideas to the solution of social, economic, environmental and political problems. We base our thinking and actions on the awareness that all phenomena are interconnected and that we are all embedded in the cyclical processes of nature.

Fellowship for Intentional Community
15 Sun Street
Stelle, IL 60919
(815) 256-2252

The Fellowship for Intentional Community (FIC), was established to gather and distribute information, conduct conferences and seminars, and to develop networks of individuals, communities, and organizations interested in intentional communities in order to facilitate greater public awareness of the opportunities these thousands of communities provide for accelerated personal growth, community development, and peaceful global transformation. The FIC includes representatives of: Community Service Inc., Community Educational Services, Inc. (CESCI), Federation of Egalitarian Communities, Earth Community Network, New England Network of Light, Inter-Communities Network, Community Publications Cooperative, National Historic Communal Societies Association, Stelle Foundation, and the Foundation for Personal and Community Development. The FIC holds an annual membership meeting and conference and offers various consulting services to individuals, communities and organizations interested in learning how to benefit from the experiences of intentional communities and cooperatives.

Fellowship of Reconciliation
Box 271
Nyack, NY 10960
(914) 358-4601

The Fellowship of Reconciliation (FOR) is an interreligious organization of pacifists. FOR seeks nonviolent solutions to conflict and seeks reconciliation through compassionate action. While it has always been vigorously opposed to war, it believes that peace is the result of justice. The FOR strives to further a social order that will utilize resources for the benefit of all, and in which no individual or group will be exploited for the profit or pleasure of others. Since its founding in 1914, the FOR has carried out a wide range of programs to promote social justice and peace.

The Focusing Institute
Contact: Gene Gendlin
410 S. Michigan Avenue
Chicago, IL 60605

In "focusing" one attends to the unclear body-sense of any situation, problem, or concern. After some minutes of physically felt unclarity, there are specific ways to let small steps of change arise from there. Usually one also gets to find out, bit by bit, more than one knew, and also more than had as yet formed or existed. The process is used in personal but also political, business, spiritual, health, and other contexts. *Focusing* (Bantam 1981) and *Let Your Body Interpret Your Dreams* (Chiron/Open Court) are two books by Gendlin on focusing.

The Institute offers workshops, a journal, and contacts in other cities.

Friends of the Third World
611 West Wayne Street
Fort Wayne, IN 46802
(219) 422-1650

Friends of the Third World is an Alternative Trading Organization based in Indiana. Friends seeks to develop production and marketing structures which promote cooperation, justice and equity between the people of the world. We operate on a nonprofit basis with both paid and volunteer staff. The "technical assistance and resource center" in Ft. Wayne, Indiana seeks to assist individuals and groups to set up "independent alternative trading projects" which are democratically managed by both consumers and producers. Educational information is also available through Whole World Books projects. Additional information and membership applications are available from the address above.

Future Survey
Contact: Michael Marien, Ed.
5413 Webster Road
LaFayette, NY 13084
(315) 677-9278

Basic documentation for the multiple perspectives on the ever-changing and ever-growing "rapids of change." Each monthly issue offers 60-70 abstracts of recent books, articles and reports on trends, forecasts, and policy proposals. Selections are made from some

150 book publishers, a score of research institutions, general interest magazines, leading newspapers, and more than 200 scholarly and professional journals. Every issue, as well as the Annual, highlights works of special originality and interest, and their interconnections. In all, more than 8,000 abstracts have been prepared since 1979.

Gesundheit Institute
Contact: Patch Adams
404 North Nelson Street
Arlington, VA 22203
(703) 525-8169

Gesundheit is a group of health professionals who have lived a 15 year experiment addressing the four major issues in health care delivery. We have never charged money, never accepted insurance reimbursement, never carried malpractice insurance, and live with our patients as friends. Our ideal patient is someone who wants a deep personal friendship for the rest of his or her life. We are now building you a free hospital in West Virginia. We need your help.

Global Education Associates
475 Riverside Drive, Suite 570
New York, NY 10115
(212) 870-3290/3291

Global Education Associates is a network of men and women in over 60 countries who share a commitment to create a more just, peaceful and human world order. We represent many diverse nationalities, cultures, religions and occupations. Our goal is to catalyze a transnational, multi-issue movement for alternatives based on the world order values of peace, social justice, ecological balance and participation in decision-making. Through its research, publications and educational programs, our associates collaborate in envisioning viable alternatives and in developing and implementing strategies for bringing those alternatives into being.

Habitat for Humanity
Contact: Millard Fuller
  or Bob Geiger
Habitat and Church Streets
Americus, GA 31709
(912) 924-6935

Nonprofit Ecumenical Christian Housing Ministry is a coalition of self-help partnership housing projects (as of 1/87, there are 171 projects in the U.S. and 34 in developing countries) based on no-profit, no-interest home construction and ownership; building decent, modest homes in partnership with people living in substandard housing.

**Heartland Center for
  Leadership Development**
P.O. Box 81806
Lincoln, NE 68501
(402) 476-3392

The Heartland Center for Leadership Development is a nonprofit corporation engaged in a variety of activities designed to help recognized and emerging leaders approach confidently the challenges associated with fundamental societal change. The Center's priorities include research on trends and policies, skill-development for community and business leadership, capacity building for community problem-solving, and clarification of emerging public policy concerns. Organizers include Milan Wall and Vicki Luther, both of whom are associated with the Center for Strategic Leadership, a Nebraska-based consulting and training organization; Robert Theobald, an Arizona-based economist and futurist; and Roger Beverage, an attorney and former director of the Nebraska Department of Banking. All four were active in the Visions From The Heartland project.

The Hesperian Foundation
Contact: Michael Blake,
    Administrative Director
P.O. Box 1692
Palo Alto, CA 94302
(415) 325-9017
    We are working to support and encourage community-run health and rehabilitation programs in rural areas of Mexico and the developing world.

**Holt Associates/Growing
    Without Schooling**
729 Boylston Street, Suite 308C
Boston, MA 02116
(617) 437-1550
    Growing Without Schooling (*GWS*) is a bi-monthly magazine for people interested in learning. Ideas on math, reading, music, art, languages, sharing work with children and recommedations for books, mag-

azines, and learning materials are included. Established in 1977 by author/educator John Holt, *GWS* is the leading source of homeschooling information in America. It contains parents' letters about taking children out of school and learning outside of school settings. *GWS* has resource lists of friendly teachers, friendly school districts, curriculum and textbook suppliers, correspondence schools, and a growing network of readers who can be contacted by others interested in homeschooling.

H.O.M.E., Inc.
Route 1
Orland, ME 04472
(207) 469-7961
    H.O.M.E., Inc., established in 1970 as a craft cooperative, is a multi-faceted organization involved in economic reconstruction and social rehabilitation through its several programs. In 1971, volunteers began a learning center to teach literacy, crafts and care of livestock. Since then, the Learning Center has grown to include a day care, adult basic education, adult education diploma courses, an alternative high school, and a college program called the Rural Education Program.

In Context
Editorial: P.O. Box 215, Sequim, WA 98382
Subscriptions: P.O. Box 2107, Sequim, WA 98382
(206) 683-4411
    In Context, a quarterly of humane sustainable culture, is

about positive, practical cultural change, as it is occurring in the world around us. Each issue focuses on a major theme, combining the personal stories of cultural pioneers with sophisticated analysis and innovative synthesis. Issue topics range from personal relations to economic systems, from how we view the Universe to how we raise our children. 64 pages with no ads. Subscriptions are $16/year.

Innovation Associates Inc.
P.O. Box 2008
Framingham, MA 01701
(617) 879-8301
Innovation Associates is a management consulting firm dedicated to building organizations that have the inspiration and ability to produce outstanding results. Clients are typically Fortune 500 companies and fast-growing mid-sized companies. The essence of the firm's work is to promote a shift from the point of view which holds people bound by current circumstances to one that empowers them to create their desired future unconstrained by their circumstances. Individuals become linked to a higher purpose common to everyone in the organization. They infuse their organization with the necessary commitment and energy to collectively realize a vision of a better world.

Institute for Community Economics
151 Montague City Road
Greenfield, MA 01301
(413) 774-7956

The Institute for Community Economics (ICE) is a nonprofit corporation providing technical and financial assistance to community land trusts, limited-equity housing coops, community loan funds, and other grassroots organizations, as well as providing information and educational material to the general public. The ICE Revolving Loan Fund, capitalized by loans and donations from concerned individuals and institutions, provides relatively short term loans to community-based groups, typically for acquisition and development of land and housing. Resources available from ICE include, *The Community Land Trust Handbook*, a slide show on community land trusts, a quarterly newsletter, and a manual on community loan fund development.

Institute for Local Self-Reliance
Contact: Larry Martin
2425 18th Street, NW
Washington, DC 20009
(202) 232-4108
The Institute for Local Self-Reliance (ILSR), a nonprofit organization established in 1974, offers a new approach to urban planning. ILSR helps cities and neighborhoods put their wealth to work, and then keeps benefits in their own communities. We analyze local economies, evaluate new technologies, and promote democratic decision-making. (Description and publications lists are available.)

Institute of Noetic Sciences
475 Gate Five Road, #300
Sausalito, CA 94965
(415) 331-5650

The Institute of Noetic Sciences is a member-supported organization whose purpose is to expand our knowledge of the nature and potentials of the mind and spirit, and to apply that knowledge to the advancement of health and well-being for humankind. (The word "noetic" comes from the Greek 'nous' meaning mind, intelligence, understanding.) The Institute is a research and educational organization which produces a variety of publications and gives a limited amount of support for leading-edge research in the forms of small grants. For a sample publication and further information contact them at the above address.

International Center for Dynamics of Development
Contact: Dana D. Reynolds
(alternate: Afif I. Tannous)
Suite 616, 4201 South 31st Street
Arlington, VA 22206
(703) 578-4627

The Center catalyzes thinking, experience, and action on Society's greatest challenge: How to Create Popular/Political Will for Orderly Change. This calls for appropriate blends of factors such as: Enlightened Heads of State; responsive government; representative political-legislative bodies; bottom-up planning for local, national, international policies; systematic orientation/education of leaders and public; fully involving women and youth; patterns to rapidly involve millions of "by-passed" people; fiscal, price, tax policies; recognition of religious values in development. The Center has focused on various problem areas: Lebanon, the Middle East, Peru, Southern Africa.

Landsman Community Services, Ltd.
375 Johnston Avenue
Courtenay, BC V9N 2Y2
Canada
(604) 338-0213/0214

Communities everywhere are both impoverished and distorted by their dependency on conventional, national currencies. Such currencies flow in and out of the community simply because money will preferably flow to the cheapest supplier, and to the greatest rate of return. This can leave the community starved for the means of exchange, often while having all the real resources at hand—people, skills, tools, materials, etc. The remedy is to establish a local currency to mobilize local resources. The Local Employment and Trading System (LETS), provides a community of almost any size with such a legal currency with a minimum of effort and expense. A general information package is available for $5, and, for $15 all the software and administration materials are available on IBM PC compatible diskettes. Some videotape material on VHS format is available for a further $20.

**Link House Peace Education and
   Resource Center**
Contact: Betty Richardson
1111 Willow Lane
Madison, WI 53706
   Link House Peace Education
and Resource Center is a service
project of the Quakers for south
central Wisconsin. Volunteers
and a fulltime director
currently provide a call-in
service for calendar clearance,
and ideas/resources to plan
events; coordinate a monthly
meeting of area groups to
strengthen bonds of cooperation
while maintaining autonomy;
send a listing of projects groups
have in the planning phase to
over 75 groups in the network;
publish an annual directory;
sponsor workshops enabling
people to work more effectively
for a just and peace-filled world
(affiliate of Interhelp); and
promote nonviolent approaches
to conflict resolution.

The Lorian Association
P.O. Box 663
Issaquah, WA 98027
(206) 392-3982
   The Lorian Assocation is a
not-for-profit educational association exploring contemporary
spirituality and the values of a
holistic world view. Our publications deal with cultural and
personal transformation, the
emergence of a global perspective, and the integration of
transpersonal development
with everyday life. We sponsor
classes and workshops, community art projects, intercultural
networking, and spiritual cele-
brations, all of which deal

either implicitly or explicitly
with the discovery of the sacra-
mental nature of our world and
the integration of an awareness
of the sacred with our daily
affairs.

Medical Self-Care
Contact: Tom Ferguson, M.D.
P.O. Box 1000
Point Reyes, CA 94956
(415) 663-8462
   Medical Self-Care is a bi-
monthly medical journal for lay-
people. We seek to provide
highly motivated self-care
practioners with tools, skills,
information, and support to
help them attain their own
health goals. In our opinion,
responsible self-care includes
keeping oneself healthy, managing illness episodes, and using
professional and lay advisors
wisely. We present both physical and psychological approaches and seek to blend the best of
orthodox professional medicine
with the most useful alternative methods. We believe
that health care is being trans-
formed as we move from an
industrial age to an information
age and that the new health
care system will be based on self-
care.

Movement for a New Society
P.O. Box 1922
Cambridge, MA 02238
   Movement for a New
Society (MNS) is a U.S.-based
organization of radical activists dedicated to creating a new
society through non-violent
revolution. We see ourselves as
part of the revolutionary tradi-

tion that includes Gandhi's successful nonviolent campaign for the national liberation of India, as well as many progressive movements in this country. MNS was founded in 1971 by women and men who saw the need for mutual support in the life-long effort to change themselves and the world around them. We are a small, member-controlled network with strong transnational ties. MNS members work on many different issues. We welcome your inquiries.

Nacul Architectural Center
Contact: Tullio Inglese
592 Main Street
Amherst, MA 01002
(413) 256-8025

Architecture has finally become an environmental science rooted in the fundamental principles of ecology, that is, plant and animal morphology which forms the rational basis for evolution. Architecture is unbiased. It utilizes labor and materials optimally, to produce energy efficient, aesthetic enclosures not for a chosen few, but for all. Architecture transcends materials and methods (technology); it transforms sticks and stones into comfortable, inspiring places in which to work and live. Architecture is the natural link between the material and spiritual worlds—a logical step and means of sustaining evolution in a positive direction. Our work includes: 1) architectural design services for residential and commercial buildings (Nacul Design Associates); 2) research in roots, principles, and implications of "ecological architecture" (Nacul Institute); and 3) building construction (Nacul Master Builders).

National Coalition of Alternative Community Schools
RD1, Box 378
Glenmoore, PA 19343
(215) 458-5138

Founded in 1976, the National Coalition of Alternative Community Schools (NCACS) is the only national (and now international) alternative school organization. It consists of several hundred independent and public alternative schools. To be a voting member a school must be non-discriminatory and participant controlled. Home schoolers are also welcomed. Anyone may become an associate member or get a subscription to the newsletter, the NCACS Journal *SKOLE*, or the national alternative school directory. There is a yearly national conference as well as several regional conferences. Jerry Mintz is the current Executive Director, its first full-time director. Sandra Hurst is current president.

The Neighborhood Works
Contact: Thom Clark, Editor
570 West Randolph Street
Chicago, IL 60606-2205
(312) 454-0126

The Neighborhood Works is an award-winning monthly news journal of resources for urban communities. Though it covers Chicago neighborhoods most intensively, its readership over ten years of publication is national. The publication regularly covers housing, energy, jobs, food, and environmental issues through the eyes of community-based organizations seeking and taking key roles in economic development. It is published by the Center for Neighborhood Technology, a nonprofit technical assistance agency involved with energy research, conservation retrofits, industrial job retention and public policy analysis. One year (10 issues) subscription is $18.

The Network Inc. of America
Contact: Mary Patricia Voell
819 North Marshall
Milwaukee, WI 53202
(414) 289-7774

The Network Inc. of America (TNIA) is an information search corporation answering both high-tech and high-touch information needs. TNIA refines, interprets, expands and organizes the information. Our product is information accessed and distributed through the network process. TNIA is a for-profit corporation. It has been our experience in building a profit based company in the information industry that "a tangible" product must be defined, marketed and delivered for your clients/customers/members to accept "networks" as legitimate communication vehicles and take advantage of its services. The Network is seeking interested companies to build local TNIA affiliates; we will share our knowledge and experience as consultants to potential network offices. Contact TNIA for support, insight or input.

The Networking Institute
296 Newton Street, Suite 350
Waltham, MA 02154
(617) 891-4727

Founded in 1982 by Jessica Lipnack and Jeffrey Stamps, after the Doubleday publication of their book, *Networking: The First Report and Directory*, The Networking Institute (TNI) is a research and consulting company. Innovators from many professions, with a variety of special interests, join The Networking Institute ($75/year) to stay connected with state-of-the-art information about how to improve their organizations, broaden their networks, and increase the effectiveness of their work. Electronic networking services, seminars, books and publications on networking are available from TNI.

New Alchemy Institute
237 Hatchville Road
East Falmouth, MA 02536
(617) 563-2655

The New Alchemy Institute, founded in 1969 in San Diego, California, promotes ecologically sound strategies for meeting basic human needs for food, energy, shelter and waste management. The Institute seeks to merge ecological priorities with marketplace demands, developing gardens, greenhouses, houses and small farm systems that are cost-effective, energy-efficient, replicable, and simple to manage. The Institute's primary audiences are gardeners, homeowners, builders, and small-scale farmers as well as children, students, and teachers. Since 1971, the Institute has occupied a 12-acre former dairy farm in East Falmouth, on Cape Cod, Massachusetts.

New Horizons for Learning

Contact: Dee Dickinson
P.O. Box 51140
Seattle, WA 98115-1140
(206) 621-7609

New Horizons for Learning is an international human resource network created to communicate an expanded vision of education. The network focuses on increasing awareness of human capabilities and offering effective methods to develop these capabilities more fully through: synthesizing and communicating information from curent research on brain/mind function; offering teaching and learning strategies based on this research, for use at all age levels and in all settings; and vitalizing the learning process for students of all age and ability levels through methods which engage the whole mind/body system.

New Options Newsletter

Contact: Mark Satin
P.O. Box 19324
Washington, DC 20036
(202) 822-0929

New Options has been called "the most intriguing political newsletter in Washing-ton" (by Art Levine of *the Washington Monthly*). It investigates new ideas and approaches that go beyond those of the traditional left and right. Recent issues have explored such topics as the "third force" in Central America, the other ("deeper") abortion debate, self-reliant local development, alternatives to full employment, and the "common ground" approach to peace. Each issue re-interprets current events, looks constructively-critically at social change groups and political books, and includes a fairly brutal "Forum" in which the new post-liberal, post-socialist ideas are debated by the readers. Monthly, $25/year; $12.50/year first year to readers of this listing.

Noren Institute

62 Stanton Street
San Francisco, CA 94114

In our fourth year now, with over 100 alumni, Noren Institute is a partnership between Andora Freeman, Michael Phillips and Claude Whitmyer, created to provide access for all people in business to the experience of the Briarpatch Society. Noren Institute offers support services to small businesses and community organizations that are entrepreneurial in nature. The Institute engages in research, training and consulting on the use of strategies that incorporate creativity and risk taking in a context of self-reliance and social-responsibility. Honesty, openness, community service and sharing of resources are encouraged as superior strategies for long term entrepreneurial success. Twice per year, in March and October, the Institute sponsors "Business Learning Teams" in "Running a One Person Business," "Marketing Without Advertising," "Honest Management I" (which focuses on personnel management) and "Honest Management II" (which focuses on issues of growth and size as well as contemporary management theory). The Learning Team format includes visits to Briarpatch businesses that highlight the Learning Team content and provide students a chance to actually discuss relevant issues with the business owners themselves. "Noren" is Japanese for the flag that hangs in the entrance to a Japanese store when it is open for business.

North American Bioregional Congress
Contact: Jacqueline Froelich
P.O. Box 104
Eureka Springs, AR 72632
(501) 253-6866

North American Bioregional Congress (NABC) is a major convening of representatives of the continental Bioregionalist Movement, to include the movements of political ecology/green politics, "deep ecology," and sustainability, along with native and tribal organizations. NABC participants not only network and congress, but also share the culture and history of the bioregions represented; help unify the bioregional movement; explore the great

common ground between bioregionalist and indigenous peoples; seed new bioregional congresses/councils, and organizations; help focus green movement political energies towards new coalitions and impact on existing political/electoral systems; and celebrate North America, Turtle Island. NABC is held every other year, in a different host bioregion, after the harvest.

Northwest Regional Foundation
Contact: Robert Stilger
East 525 Mission
Spokane, WA 99202
(509) 484-6733

Northwest Regional Foundation (N.R.F.) is a nonprofit corporation engaged in a wide variety of community improvement efforts. In addition to citizen participation, community education, housing assistance and nonprofit capacity building work in Spokane, NRF also offers program design, management and evaluation services to other communities and organizations.

Ozark Area Community Congress
Contact: Jacqueline Froelich
P.O. Box 104
Eureka Springs, AR 72632
(501) 253-6866

The Ozark Area Community Congress (OACC) has had yearly convenings since October, 1980. Citizens who have been concerned about environmental and political aspects of life in the Ozarks have attended to testify on behalf of their individual and community interests. Most of those who have responded to a bioregional congress call are working from an ecological base in the following areas: conservation and environmental protection, organic agriculture/permaculture, peace, sustainable economics and business, renewable resource development, holistic health and education, media and communications, water quality, land stewardship, "all-species" rights, forest husbandry, and appropriate technology.

Pacific Rim Futuring Institute
Antioch University
1165 Eastlake Avenue East
Seattle, WA 98109
(206) 343-1521
The Pacific Rim Futuring Institute offers a graduate program leading to a masters degree in Whole Systems Design with an emphasis in futuring and systems change. This two-year program is weekend based. The Institute also offers conferences, seminars, and consulting referrals. The Whole Systems Design program of Antioch University Seattle, offers additional degree programs in Organization Systems Renewal as well as individualized areas of concentration. The heart of all programs is a systemic perspective.

Peacework
Contact: Pat Farren, Editor
American Friends Service
  Committee
2161 Massachusetts Avenue

Cambridge, MA 02140
(617) 661-6130
Peacework is A New England Peace and Social Justice Newsletter published by the regional office of the American Friends Service Committee. This 16-page monthly provides news, ideas, and experiences of people helping us move to life-sacred values for the 21st century, with an ethic of reconciliation and nonviolence and a focus on movement-building and the spiritual roots of speaking truth to power. Sample copy free. Published regularly since 1972.

Planet Drum
P.O. Box 31251
San Francisco, CA 94131
(415) 285-6556
Planet Drum Foundation developed the concept of a bioregion in response to the need for an effective grassroots approach for making considerations of sustainability, community self-determination, regional self-reliance, and ecological imperatives more prominent as goals of social and political change. Since 1974 Planet Drum has communicated these ideas through organizing meetings, talks, workshops, four books, six regional "bundles" of information, and a tri-annual newspaper *Raise the Stakes*. Its steadily growing membership includes community and environmental activists, alternative energy and anti-nuclear adherents, Native American and resources defense groups, permaculture (sustainable agriculture) and planning practitioners,

progressive issues advocates, and interested individuals ranging from educators to forest workers. They are located in all the states of the U.S. and provinces of Canada, and in South America, Europe, Japan and Australia. Membership and publications information is available by sending a self addressed stamped envelope to the address above.

Planetary Citizens
P.O. Box 710037
San Jose, CA 95171-0037
(408) 253-7970

Planetary Citizens includes the people from most parts of the world and from all walks of life—industrial workers, homemakers, astronauts, government officials, farmers, doctors, lawyers, teachers, artists and world leaders. They share a global view which goes beyond racial, religious, and political beliefs. Planetary Citizens was formed in 1972 and incorporated in 1974, with Norman Cousins and former Secretary-General of the UN, U Thant as Honorary Co-Chairman. Planetary Citizens has Non-Governmental accreditation at the United Nations. It is incorporated as a not-for-profit organization.

The Project on the Vietnam Generation
Contact: Sandie Fauriol,
   Executive Director
554 National Press Building
Washington, DC 20045
(202) 783-0088

The Project on the Vietnam Generation's mission is to serve as a catalyst to help our generation lessen the damaging effects of the Vietnam era and to realize its full potential through the year 2030 as leaders, stewards, and citizens of our country and the world. The Project fosters scholarships, public education and dialogue on the dynamics, goals, and achievements of the Vietnam Generation through the year 2030. We accomplish this through an international network, publication of a quarterly newsletter called *Report,* by conducting surveys on generational activities, and through Study Groups that examine issues related to the Vietnam era and generation.

Public Interest Media Project
Contact: Stan Pokras
P.O. Box 14066
Philadelphia, PA 19123
(215) 922-0227

For over 15 years, the Media Project has been active locally, nationally and internationally to promote new forms and flows of information, especially group (many-to-many) communication. Our occasional newsletter, *Other Networks,* is one of the very few sources of general news in this field. The Media Project works throughout the Delaware Valley to teach group communication through the mail, via computer bulletin boards and computer conferencing systems. We provide computer support and training to nonprofit organizations, and computerized typesetting for local newsletters as well as the national newspaper, *Green Action.* We have taught the many-to-many process used by Action Linkage to more than a dozen separate organizations. The Media Project needs volunteers to write reviews and articles about useful publications and organizations. As reviewers of alternative literature, we have collected a library with examples of over 600 alternative publications. Volunteers help maintain our huge flow of information in an orderly fashion, and are provided training in the use of computers as well as given access to our equipment for projects of their own. We have eight computers (including two MacIntoshes) and a high quality copy machine. You can help! Please call.

Relationship First, Inc.
(Formerly Trusteeship Institute, Inc.)
Contact: Terry Mollner
Baker Road
Shutesbury, MA 01072
(413) 259-1600
Relationship First, Inc. (RF) consults to firms forming as or converting to worker-owned cooperatives based on the Mondragon model. It's new book, *Mondragon: Beyond Capitalism and Socialism,* argues that "a third way" opposite to both capitalism and socialism based on quantum physics is emerging everywhere. RF runs free weekend training to teach this at the level of interpersonal experience and then assists a local group to create a branch of RF

Federal Credit Union and build a local Mondragon.

Search for Common Ground
1701 K Street, NW, Suite 403
Washington, DC 20006
(202) 835-0777
Search for Common Ground, a non-partisan, nonprofit organization based in Washington, DC, is dedicated to bringing about a fundamental shift in the way nations act so that international security is assured. It is responding to the challenge by organizing programs designed to promote fresh and innovative approaches on security issues. As its name indicates, Search for Common Ground promotes action based on what unites individuals, organizations, and nations—not on what separates them. It believes the nuclear age has made obsolete the idea that countries can "win" their security at the expense of others. It is determined to move beyond adversarial thinking—beyond either "us-against-the-Russians" or "us-against-the-Pentagon" perspectives.

TRANET
P.O. Box 567
Rangeley, ME 04970-0567
(207) 864-2252
TRANET is a transnational network of, by and for people who are helping one another to change the world by changing their own life styles. It is a network in as much as there is no center. Each member is fully autonomous linking for mutual-aid as need and opportunity

arise. The TRANET switchboard in Rangeley is merely a linking operation, helping members with offers to find members with needs. TRANET is transnational in as much as it sees people-to-people networks taking the place of governments and ameliorating competition and the trend to war inherent in a world governance based on Nation-States. (Membership $30/year—includes a subsidy for a Third World member.)

Transformation Research Network
Contact: Ruben Nelson
134 Monterey Drive
Nepean, Ontario K2H 7A8
Canada
(613) 236-9712

Transformation Research Network (TRN) is a Canadian network founded to find, link and support persons/organizations who want to understand, respond positively to and even give thanks for the profound changes taking place within and among us. Our premise is that Canada is already becoming one of the world's first postmodern, postindustrial countries; and that this transition needs to be understood so that our good intentions and our efforts, both personal and organizational, are actually aligned with the emerging future. We publish an occasional newsletter, and organize elegant national conferences. Average donation: $40/year.

The Trinity Forum for International Security and Conflict Resolution
Contact: Bruce M. Berlin, Executive Director
P.O. Box 8636
Santa Fe, NM 87504
(505) 473-4298

Named after the world's first test of an atomic bomb, The Trinity Forum serves as a center for dialogue on peace and security questions. The Forum brings together people with widely diverse perspectives on these issues. It offers a non-partisan mechanism for engaging both the defense establishment and the disarmament movement in the peace and security dialogue. Its goal is to promote the resolution of issues through a process of dialogue that embraces the relative truths of different positions on international security and world peace so that a new vision of global security and understanding can emerge.

The Water Center
Contact: Barbara Harmony
P.O. Box 548
Eureka Springs, AR 72632
(501) 253-9755/9431

The Water Center gathers, distills and disseminates information on water issues emphasizing personal responsibility for human and hazardous wastes. Their provocative 92 page book *We All Live Downstream* contains information on the water crisis, current composter information, conservation and community action. This profusely illustrated handbook provides concise personal and cultural strategies for protecting water resources. We are available to talk or consult on all these topics.

Windstar Foundation
Box 286
Snowmass, CO 81654
(303) 927-4777
Windstar is a nonprofit foundation begun in 1976 by John Denver and Thomas Crum. Windstar provides a global community-at-large with vital information towards a peaceful, sustainable future through the annual Choices for the Future Symposium, quarterly *Windstar Journal*, audio and video productions, and Biodome Project (a solar-heated dome-greenhouse). Retreat experiences and educational programs in conflict resolution, citizen diplomacy, renewable energy, food production, land stewardship, global resource management, and personal growth are offered on Windstar's 1000 acre Rocky Mountain home. Windstar welcomes your participation in programs. Membership ($35 annually) includes *Windstar Journal* (subscriptions $18 annually), and local sponsorship of Windstar presentations.

The World Food Assembly
Contact: Mr. Robin Sharp
5, Harrowby Court
Harrowby Street
London W1H 5FA, England
(01) 262-6969
The World Food Assembly is a coalition of independent groups and people from all parts of the world, united in the conviction that radical changes are needed if we are to meet our human responsibility of ensuring food for all. Our coalition encompasses a wide spectrum of people's movements in more than 60 countries. We are small farmers, rural women, development workers, peasants, environmentalists, trade unionists, researchers, priests, journalists, nutritionists, and people working in the fields of appropriate technology, human rights and alternative lifestyles. In coming together to make common cause on what we regard as the fundamental moral issues on food and justice, we believe our coalition can be an important force for change.

World Future Society
Contact: Sally Cornish
4916 St. Elmo Avenue
Bethesda, MD 20814
(301) 656-8274
The World Future Society acts as a neutral clearinghouse and forum for people interested in the future. Our aim is to help people of all political and social views, ideologies, and nationalities to share their ideas relating to the human future. We have about 25,000 members and subscribers in 80 countries. We have no prerequisite for membership and dues are kept modest ($25/year) so that anyone seriously interested in the future can join. We publish a magazine *The Futurist*, which goes to all our members. In addition, we publish a scholarly journal *Futures Research*

Quarterly and a newsletter *Future Survey* which each month summarizes the most significant books and articles dealing with public issues. We hold conferences and have chapters so members can meet face-to-face.

World Peace Center
Contact: Don Tilley
P.O. Box 95062
Lincoln, NE 68509
(402) 466-6622 or 476-7398

The World Peace Center plans to establish a large exhibition center by 1992 on I-80 near Lincoln, Nebraska, which will graphically depict new visions about living together in peace and practical ways for bringing about this transformation. Four areas necessary for peace will be the focus of interactive simulations/ exhibits: 1) integration of self, 2) applications of nurturing skills to home/community, 3) becoming one people on earth (global family of families), and 4) developing an ecology which represents earth as a "living organism." There are a variety of programs for outreach in addition to the planned exhibits.

World Peace University
35 S.E. 60th Avenue
Portland, OR 97215
(503) 231-3771

The program of the World Peace University brings together advanced communications technology and dynamic human interaction in an educational setting that speaks to the world in a positive and creative way. The Internship Program accepts persons who desire to become world citizen diplomats for a core study program which focuses on peace studies, personal development and consciousness raising, and telecommunications. The two phases are divided into two fifteen-week sessions followed by an individual project. Interns come from all parts of the globe. Radio for Peace, an international short wave radio station, is being developed in cooperation with the University for Peace, Costa Rica.

OOO

Resources and References

Whether you're just beginning the journey or whether your hunger for new ideas has been longstanding, this section is designed to provide leads to periodicals and organizations active in the many areas of social entrepreneurship. This resource list includes organizations and publications that are changing thinking and action in a broad range of areas.

Resources are organized by the sections in the text to which their activity most closely relates; obviously, many groups could have been listed under a number of headings, and we have used our best judgment in our choices. For contact information and a description of an individual organization or periodical, see Appendix A: Social Entrepreneurs.

The creation of this resource list was extraordinarily difficult for many reasons.

First, there are far more creative and positive organizations than can possibly be listed without overload—and new ones are appearing constantly. Choices have been made in collaboration with those who helped create the book but we look forward to receiving suggestions for groups that could be added to future editions.

Second, we tried to balance those primarily concerned with knowledge and learning with those involved in action—and of course, include those that are balanced in both.

Third, since most of the readers of this edition will be in North America, many fine groups outside North America were excluded. For tapping the wealth of activity around the world, TRANET, Internation Center for Dynamics of Development, and Friends of the Third World should be your starting point. As translations are made or printings created in other parts of the world, we hope to develop suitable lists for those readers.

Fourth, for those who want to get a sense of the best new books coming out, see the annual book awards from New Options (listed in Appendix A).

If *Rapids* moves you to believe that you can be your own heroine or hero and can make a difference, then it will have been a success. Cultures change not because one great person demands that they do but rather because many individuals decide to act in slightly different ways. You will have learned from *Rapids* that there are no reliable formulas and no slick models which ensure effectiveness. Rather, your personal sincerity and openness will be *your* effective qualities.

You can have the most impact in your own established circles: your school or college, your church or synagogue, your circle of colleagues and friends, your local council or school board. We hope this listing will provide resources that can be appropriately used with your groups. Pick and choose those resources which seem most valuable to you. Don't try and get involved with all of them!

SECTION 1. *The Images of Change*

Organizations:
World Future Society.

Publications:
The Aquarian Conspiracy, Marilyn Ferguson, J. P. Tarcher, 1980, $9.95; the very influential book which introduced many people to the need for new thinking. *At the Crossroads*, pamphlet (slide-tape presentation also available), Communications Era Task Force, Box 2240, Wickenburg, AZ 85358, 1984, $4; a brief description of the reality in which we are now living. *Future Survey*—see Appendix A. *An Incomplete Guide to the Future*, Willis W. Harman, Norton, 1979, $5.95; challenged people to new thinking and still does so— one of my two key short books for widening one's understanding. *Megatrends: Ten New Directions Transforming Our Lives*, John Naisbitt, 6th edition, Warner, 1983, $4.50; helped many people see

the rapidity of change in world culture. *New Options*—see Appendix A. *New Rules: Searching for Self-Fulfillment in a World Turned Upside Down,* Daniel Yankelovich, Random, 1981, $15.95; an examination of the extent to which new styles have permeated the American culture. *Player Piano,* Kurt Vonnegut, Dell, 1986, $9.95; one of the science-fiction books which shows the negative potentials in apparently positive dynamics. *The Third Wave,* Alvin Toffler, Bantam, 1981, $4.95; another of the books which helped wake America up to the certainty of a different future. *The Triple Revolution,* Ad Hoc Committee on the Triple Revolution, 1964; copies available for $4 from Box 2240, Wickenburg, AZ 85358; the document which started much of the fundamental change discussion in the United States. *The Universe is a Green Dragon,* Brian Swimme, Bear & Co., 1984; a reexamination of our place in the cosmos.

SECTION 2. *Beyond the Rapids*

Organizations:

The Bicycle Network, Chinook Learning Center, Choosing our Future, Co-op America, East Bay Briarpatch Network, Gesundheit Institute, Habitat for Humanity, Holt Associates/Growing Without Schooling, H.O.M.E. Inc., Landsman Community Services, Lorian Association, NACUL Architecture Center, National Coalition of Alternative Community Schools, New Alchemy Institute, Noren Institute, Relationship First, Inc., The Water Center, and World Peace University.

Publications:

Beyond Adversary Democracy, Jane J. Mansbridge, University of Chicago Press, 1980, $14; what it would mean for people to work together in democratic systems. *Beyond Despair,* Robert Theobald, Metamorphous Press, 1986, $9.95; an examination of new social systems and life-styles. *Beyond the Commission Reports: The Coming Crisis in Education,* Linda Darling-Hammond, Rand Corporation, 1700 Main Street, Box 2138, Santa Monica, CA 90406, 1984, $4; a discussion of the inevitability of a very severe shortage of teachers. *Catalyst*—see Appendix A. *The Churchman/Human Quest*—see Appendix A. *Darkness and Scattered Light,* William Irwin Thompson, Anchor, 1978; poetic discussion of the dynamics of cultures as they face the challenges of the futures. *Diet for a Small Planet,* Frances Moore Lappe, Ballantine, 1982, $3.50; the book which opened up the issue of the appropriate level at which one should eat on the food chain. *Future Work: Jobs, Self-Employment and Leisure After the Industrial Era*, James Robertson, Universe Books, 1985, $17.50; how can and should work be organized in our new conditions. *The Critical Path*, R. Buckminster Fuller, St. Martin's Press, 1982, $10.95; the choices we must make if we are to create the high quality of life which lies within our grasp. *Green Politics: The Global Promise*, Charlene Spretnak and Fritjof Capra, Bear and Company, 1986, $8.95; an examination of the meaning of the German green politics movement and its applicability in North America. *The Guaranteed Income*, Edited by Robert Theobald, Doubleday, 1967; out of print; an examination of alternative ways of distributing income. *High-Level Wellness*, Edited by Donald B. Ardell, Rodale Press, 1977; out of print; thinking about being well rather than being sick. *How Children Learn*, John Holt, Dell, 1986, $7.95; Holt observes and comments on the natural learning processes through which children explore, experiment and play. *Life or Work: Meaningful Employment in an Age of Limits*, William A. Charland, Jr., Crossroad/Continuum, 1987, $15.95; title good description of contents. *Medical Self-Care*—see Appendix A. *Mondragon: Beyond Capitalism and Socialism*, Terry Mollner, New Society Publishers, 1986; an examination of the potential of a work system developed among the Basques to inspire new directions in the rich countries. *New Horizons for Learning*—see Appendix A. *On Death and Dying*, Elizabeth Kubler-Ross, Macmillan, 1970, $4.95; moving beyond the western fear of death. *The Phenomenom of Man*, Teilhard de Chardin, Harper and Row, 1955; an examination of our emerging world. *The Sane Alternative: A Choice of Futures*, James Robertson, 3rd edition, River Basin Publishing Company, 1983, $4.95; the type of world we need in order to ensure our survival. *To Have or To Be?* Erich Fromm, Bantam, 1981, $4.50; the choice between two very different ways of living.

SECTION 3. Leadership Patterns in the Rapids

Organizations:

Heartland Center for Leadership Development, Innovation Associates, The Network Inc. of America, and TRANET.

Publications:

Beyond Power, Marilyn French, Ballantine, 1986, $11.95; an analysis of the conceptual and structural basis of today's world.

The Change Masters: Innovation for Productivity in the American Corporation, Rosabeth Moss Kanter, Simon and Shuster, 1985, $9.95; how to manage the change process in business. *In Search of Excellence: Lessons from America's Best Run Companies*, Thomas J. Peters and Robert H. Waterman, Warner, 1984, $8.95. *The Knowledge Executive: Leadership in an Information Society*, Harlan Cleveland, Truman Talley/Dutton, 1985, $18.95; changing patterns of leadership in a new world. *Leaders: The Strategies of Taking Charge*, Warren Bennis and Bert Nanus, Harper and Row, 1985, $19.45; demystifies the art of leadership. *Servant Leadership: A Journey into the Nature of Legitimate Power and Greatness*, Robert K. Greenleaf, Paulist Press, 1977, $8.95; one of the classics in leadership literature and a source of inspiration to me personally. *Synergic Power: Beyond Domination Beyond Permissiveness*, James H. and Marguerite Craig, 2nd edition, ProActive Press, 1979, $6.95; a re-examination of the nature of power and authority and how to use them effectively rather than destructively.

SECTION 4. *The Scales of Change*

Organizations:

Association for Humanistic Psychology, Animal Town Game Company, The Bicycle Network, Center for Supportive Community, Center for Urban Education, Connect/US-USSR, Co-Op America, Earthstewards Network, Fellowship for Intentional Community, The Focusing Institute, Habitat for Humanity, Institute for Community Economics, Institute for Local Self-Reliance, Link House, North American Bioregional Congress, Northwest Regional Foundation, Ozark Area Community Congress, Planet Drum, Planetary Citizens, and World Peace Center.

Publications:

Cities and the Wealth of Nations: Principles of Economic Life, Jane Jacobs, Random House, 1985, $4.95; argues that centralized nation-states destroy local economies. *Communities*—see Appendix A. *Community is Possible: Repairing America's Roots*, Harry C. Boyte, Harper and Row, 1984, $6.95; the importance community could regain in America's patterns. *Deep Ecology: Living As If Nature Mattered*, Bill Devall and George Sessions, Gibbs M. Smith, 1985, $15.95; the constraints we must observe if the planet is to survive into the indefinite future. *Design with Nature*, Ian L. McHarg, American Planning Association, 1969, $6.95; learning to work with ecological forces rather than against them. *Dwellers in the Land*, Kirkpatrick Sale, Sierra, 1985, $14.95; a clear-cut statement of the anti-authoritarian, anti-technology, radical decentralist vision. *Focusing*, Eugene T. Gendlin, Bantam, 1981, $4.50; set of techniques which permit people to discover how they think by interacting intensively with another person. *Frogs into Princes: Neuro Linguistic Programming*, Richard Bandler and John Grinder, Real People Press, 1979, $6.50; how we prevent ourselves from developing our real potentials. *Gaia: A New Look at Life on Earth*, J. E. Lovelock, Oxford University Press, 1979, $6.95; to what extent is it useful to think of planet earth as a living organism. *The Healing Web: Social Networks and Human Survival*, Marc Pilisuk and Susan Parks, University Press of New England, 1986, $21.50; examines the possible extension of non-kinship ties into the traditional definitions of the family. *Neighborhood Works*—see Appendix A. *Ourselves and Our Children: A Book By And For Parents*, The Boston Women's Health Book Collective, Random House, 1978, $15.95; examining what it means to care for children in today's world. *Peace: A Dream Unfolding*, Edited by Patrick Crean and Penney Kome, Sierra Club Books, 1986, $18.95; an illustrated compendium of the forces which are driving us to understand the full meaning of peace. *Peacework*—see Appendix A. *The Possible Human: A Course In Extending Your Physical, Mental and Creative Abilities*, Jean Houston, J. P. Tarcher, 1982, $9.95; the title says it all! *Toward a Human World Order: Beyond the National Security Straitjacket*, Gerald and Patricia Mische, Paulist Press, 1977, $4.95; what it would mean to move beyond thinking in nation-state terms. *Toward a Psychology of Being*, Abraham Maslow, 2nd edition, Van Nostrand, Reinhold, 1968, $8.50; one of the pioneering works in changing our patterns of thought from objectivity to new understandings of the power of the mind.

SECTION 5. *The Skills of Change*

Organizations:

Center for Non-Violent Communication, and Institute of Noetic Sciences.

Publications:

Black Elk Speaks, John C. Neihardt, University of Nebraska Press, 1979, $16.50; a Sioux Indian tells his own fascinating personal history and thereby introduces us to the traditional life of his people. *Brain-Mind Bulletin*—see Appendix A. *The Evolutionary Journey: A Personal Guide to a Positive Future*, Barbara Marx Hubbard, Mindbody, 1985, $7.95; a guide to changing perceptions of reality. *Higher Creativity: Liberating the Unconscious for Breakthrough Insights*, Willis Harman and Howard Rheingold, J.P. Tarcher, 1984, $8.95; a challenge to objective patterns of analysis and thinking. *In Context. A New Science of Life*, Rupert Sheldrake, J.P. Tarcher, 1983, $7.95; argues that the process of learning itself changes the world in which we live. *The Tao of Physics*, Fritjof Capra, Bantam, 1977, $4.95; shows how knowledge in physics meshes with our emerging understandings of personal and social behavior.

SECTION 6. Managers of Crisis

Organizations:
Cultural Exchange Service, Friends of the Third World, The Hesperian Foundation, International Center for Dynamics of Development, Pacific Rim Futuring Institute, and World Food Assembly.

Publications:
International Debt Crisis, The Debt Crisis Network, Institute for Policy Studies, 1985, $3.95; describes the dangers of our current situation and the opportunities for dealing with them. *Pacific Shift*, William Irwin Thompson, Sierra Club Books, 1986, $15.95; the shifting geographical and philosophical balance in the world.

SECTION 7. Putting It All Together

Organizations:
Action Linkage (see Appendix C), Consultants for a Positive Future, Elmwood Institute, Fellowship of Reconciliation, Movement for a New Society, The Project on the Vietnam Generation, Search for Common Ground, The Networking Institute, Transformation Research Network, Trinity Forum, and Windstar Foundation.

Publications:
Development as Social Transformation, Herb Addo, et al., Westview Press, 1986, $28.50; genuine development must be persued against the grain of the current world system. *Free Spaces: The*

Sources of Democratic Change in America, Sara M. Evans and Harry C. Boyte, Harper and Row, 1987, $6.95; processes by which change can be created through open discussion. *Getting to Yes: Negotiating Agreement Without Giving In,* Roger Fisher and William Ury, Penguin, 1983, $5.95; alternatives to violence in the negotiating process. *This Way Daybreak Comes: Women's Values and the Future,* Anne Cheatham and Mary Clare Powell, New Society Publishers, 1986, $12.95; examines the thesis that women's values can be critical to a positive future.   OOO

Action Linkage

Action Linkage is the oldest general purpose networking organization in the United States and possibly in the world which is designed to support fundamental change. I started the organization in 1969; it has gone through a number of name and style changes to keep up with the ever-changing dynamics.

Action Linkage encourages, supports and inspires free and open discussion about the problems and possibilities of rapid change as well as the challenges which are obvious once one recognizes the existence of limits. It does all of its work in a context which stresses the importance of values.

Specific activities of Action Linkage include:
• operating discussion groups and task groups by mail for general and specific fields, and circulating the results of the groups;
• training editors and disseminating information on how to operate mail discussion groups;
• encouraging face-to-face discussion groups by providing low-cost support materials to both groups and individuals;
• publishing a newsletter giving an overview of Action Linkage's activities.

Ann Weiser, coordinator, has been called "one of the pioneers of paper-based conferencing" for her role in creating these by-mail discussion groups.

When this work creates practical and workable models or solutions, they are published in an open-ended form—along with contact people and organizations—that encourages readers to think for themselves and to find their own truth and direction. When models are applied, we let people know about both the positive and the negative results. We emphasize the creation and distribution of *knowledge* rather than information. We recognize that facts emerge from a particular vision of the universe rather than being relevant for all time.

For example, when I was first working on the manuscript that eventually became *Rapids*, I invited people in Action Linkage to comment on drafts of the book. More than 250 members participated in a process which so greatly improved the book, it can appropriately be called ours, rather than mine.

Members of Action Linkage see each other as autonomous human beings and aim to avoid controlling each other's actions. We seek ways to be effective in our personal worlds by learning to be the types of change agents and social entrepreneurs described in this book. Perhaps our most important service is helping people recognize where their colleagues are struggling to discover new realities and patterns.

Some portraits of potential Action Linkage members will help you decide whether this activity will suit you.

June, in her late 20's, is currently living with her fourth roommate. She is frustrated and angry because, as she puts it:

> There's got to be a better way! We don't often get beyond talking about clothes and videos and boyfriends but when we do it seems my friends are as frustrated as I am. But when I talk about values, about wanting to live in a community where people care for

each other, they see me as naive and unrealistic. What is worse, so do I. What I want to find is a group where the people have their feet on the ground as well as their heads in the clouds.

Karl, 36, is dissatisfied with his job. And he doesn't think that another job switch will get at the root of his dissatisfaction. He'd like to be his own boss and contribute to the welfare of the community by his activities:

I was talking about this TV show with some guys at work the other day. It showed how many people were starting their own businesses and co-ops. We'd like to evaluate the possibilities but we don't know where to start.

Candace, in her 40's, works for the community health services but she's tired of working to cure sick people:

We know so much about healthy lifestyles and wellness; why don't we emphasize that instead of coping with illness when it appears as a result of a dangerous life-style. There must be other people who think this way but it's hard to find them. And the obstacles seem so huge. Where can we start?

Bryant, 50, has devoted his life to education but he's getting very close to burnout:

We're getting criticism from everywhere. Everybody has his own pet cure but nobody seems to want to look at the basis for our difficulties. I'm going to have to quit if I can't find a group of peers who have accepted the need for real change and are talking about what we can do in practical terms.

Elizabeth is well known in her community for her quiet and effective work over the last thirty years. She has good friends and strong contacts. She is proud of her community because it dealt with the trauma of the last twenty years as well as anywhere, but in private she will say:

Our past successes are being swallowed up by new developments. None of us seems to have any sort of handle on how to manage the new issues. I suspect that there are people out there who could help but I don't know how to connect my network with the new knowledge.

Joseph and Alice are retired and they are spending their time on the issues which really matter to them. They've always been drawn to working on peace and environment questions. But Joseph hasn't yet found the place to connect:

There seem to be so many groups working on pieces of the puzzle. If I've learned anything through my life, it's that everything is connected to everything else. I want to find the group that's trying to look at the whole picture even if it's not being fully successful.

Action Linkage will not shelter you from the rapids—but it will introduce you to people learning the skills needed to enjoy running them rather than being afraid of the turbulence. Action Linkage is a process and a way of interconnecting that shares skills needed to tolerate high degrees of uncertainty and encourages people to become self-starters. Action Linkage is not for those who want to be told what they should do. But if you think social change falls more or less midway between being easy and difficult, and has to be done in a context that's somewhere near the intersection of the personal and social, then Action Linkage can be the right place. But only you can decide this.

Memberships and information may be obtained from Action Linkage, 5825 Telegraph Avenue #45, Oakland, CA 94609. For memberships only, use the card in this book that includes a discount (or mention that you read about it in *The Rapids of Change)* and mail to Knowledge Systems, 7777 West Morris Street, Indianapolis, IN 46231; computer address on Econet is appcomeo.scs.   OOO

APPENDIX D

The Study Guide

The assumption behind *The Rapids of Change* is that profound, immediate shifts are taking place in the culture and that many people are aware of them. However, few places exist where we can get together to talk about our insurmountable opportunities. A print and cassette-tape study guide has been created that allows people—whether playing their personal or institutional roles—to learn how others see current realities.

Our study-group process uses a unique method to break through the masks which many of us wear. The introduction process asks people to describe three of their roles and the passion which brings them to the group. I have used this approach for several years and continue to be amazed at the enthusiasm which emerges when people are able to talk about what really matters to them rather than being stuck with conventional agendas.

I have watched the power structure of a town agree that it ought to be doing more. I have seen a group of women move more strongly into leadership roles in social change activities for a large community as they discovered that many of them saw the same need for fundamental change. I have discovered that members of groups, who believed they already knew all about each other, could be totally unaware of levels of commitment that others in the system would like to bring to their work. In short, there is considerable pent-up energy around groups that is not getting catalyzed.

After the introduction process, the study group encourages those involved to explore the book in the order they want and with the depth that seems appropriate to them. The time spent can range from a single session which covers all the materials to one meeting for each section of the book. The audio-tapes and the printed material make it possible for people to lead the group without being experts—indeed there are no experts in working with this sort of material.

It is my conviction that we are now moving back to a period of new and creative thought. Few, if any, of us can learn enough without testing our ideas on others. This study guide will challenge you without overwhelming you. I hope that you will choose to be involved.

For information, use the card included in *Rapids* or write Knowledge Systems, 7777 West Morris Street, Indianapolis, IN 46231. Computer address on Econet is appcomeo.scs.

Knowledge Systems, Inc.

Knowledge Systems, Inc. (KSI) was designed to be the link between pioneers of today's frontier and those who want to homestead the future. KSI's spiritual ancestors are the fur traders, the Lewises and Clarks, the camel caravan drivers, the merchant-sailors who opened up Europe's trade with Asia after listening to Marco Polo's wild tales from his travels.

Today's "explorers" are social entrepreneurs and they have some exciting stories to tell about life on the frontiers of health and healing, education, vocation, conflict resolution, technology, and many other areas. See Appendix A for some examples of their work.

These social entrepreneurs have learned how to combine the qualities of compassion and street savvy needed for life in our emerging global village. They seem to share a vision that the new style of work has to satisfy both the social and the spiritual dimensions of our lives and are inventing new personal, family, business, regional and global tools that will serve this insight.

Someone will someday write the definitive history of the explosion of human potential of our times. Until that work is produced, KSI will try to pass along some of the social and human implications of what the explorers see lying over the next hill.

KSI was incorporated in Indiana in 1986, and is planning its work in two areas:

1. To develop other publications which enlarge on the themes of social entrepreneurship and living effectively at the intersection of the personal and the social.

2. To create in cooperation with Action Linkage and other pragmatic idealists the knowledge system mentioned in Section 3. For now, call it a new form of encyclopedia: it helps people understand the context of the issues with which they are dealing and, therefore, enables them to ask the relevant questions that will lead to the solution or next step. The major problem the knowledge system addresses is our inability to define with sufficient clarity, both as individuals and as a society, what we want to achieve.

Finally, thank you for purchasing this book; we hope you find it useful. Please tell your friends! And if you are also excited by the challenge of our times, but clear-eyed about what we need to do and the resources and human wisdom it will take, please give us a call. Contact David Speicher at (317) 241-0749; write to 7777 West Morris Street, Indianapolis, IN 46231; or send a computer message via our Econet account, appcomeo.scs.   OOO

INDEX

academics 30, 166, 171
Achille Lauro 12
Action Linkage 22, 80, 106, 203, 204
Afghanistan 192
age groups 42; middle-aged 97, 117; teenage 61
agriculture 34, 52-53, 60, 63, 82, 103-104, 120, 161, 168, 171, 172; corporate farms 104; depression 12, 169; era 60, 82, 161; sector 34, 168, 171
AIDS 115
alcoholics 77, 180
all-win, win-win 80, 94, 95, 124; win-lose 94, 123, 186
Alternatives for Washington 117
America 20, 36, 43, 58, 63, 68, 70-73, 78, 96-97, 103-104, 114, 120-121, 123, 135, 147, 151, 157, 159, 164, 171, 173, 186, 191-192, 194-195, 197, 200, 203-204; American dream 67; Americans 12, 39, 71, 96, 130; heartland 78, 100, 118, 162; Southwest 120, 177
anthropology 60
Antioch University 190
Arab countries 74, 158
Arizona 20, 34, 185
Asia, Asians 57, 157
At the Crossroads 21, 93
Athens 71
authority 12, 18, 19, 30-34, 37, 44, 48, 54, 66, 75, 87-89, 93-95, 97-98, 105-108, 117-122, 125, 131, 150, 155, 157, 162, 179, 187-

189, 192-196, 206; bosses 58; chain of command 107; coercion 95, 98, 124; formal 106; hierarchical 85, 87; knowledge-based 63; police power 152; powerlessness 42; power over 23, 34, 106, 132, 176; sapiential 89, 108; structures 36, 105-106, 108, 146; top-down 87, 97, 106—*see also* leadership
autonomy 61, 65, 111, 119, 121

balance 12, 14, 17-18, 33, 40, 47, 48, 51, 54, 57, 112, 121, 133, 138, 158, 172, 174-175, 179-181, 189, 191, 197
Bandler, Richard 140
Basque 97, 163
Bateson, Gregory 35, 81
Bellamy, Edward 164
Bennis, Warren 91
Beyond War 80
biology 29, 92; biotechnology 34; toxins 158
biomass 196
bioregion 119-122, 125, 187, 193, 199; regional compacts, interdependence 121; system 16
birth 116; control, contraception, sterilization 53, 61, 115; defects 200; pregnancy 38
body language 145
brain 153, 189; structures 15
breakdowns, disasters, mistakes, stresses, tensions 11-15, 17-19, 22-23, 33, 38-39, 47, 51, 53, 65, 67-69, 70-71, 74, 76, 89-